WINE INVESTMENT

for

PORTFOLIO DIVERSIFICATION

*How Collecting Fine Wines
Can Yield Greater Returns
than Stocks and Bonds*

MAHESH KUMAR
BA(HONS), ACMA, ATT, CMC, MBA, DIPIC

FOREWORD BY MICHAEL BROADBENT

Other Books by The Wine Appreciation Guild

"The best wine publisher in the US."
—Edward Cointreau, Gourmand World Cookbook Award

The Wine Atlas of New Zealand by Michael Cooper
Icon: Art of the Wine Label by Jeffrey Caldewey and Chuck House
World Encyclopedia of Champagne and Sparkling Wine by Tom Stevenson
Champagne and Sparkling Wine Guide by Tom Stevenson
Portugal's Wines and Wine Makers, New Revised Edition by Richard Mason
Tokaj by Alkonyi Laszlo
Chow! Venice by Shannon Essa and Ruth Edenbaum
The New Italy by Daniele Cernelli and Marco Sabellico
Olive Oil by Leonardo Romanelli
Cheese by Gabriella Ganugi
Prosciutto by Carla Bardi
Pasta by Fabrizio Ungaro
The Wines of France by Clive Coates
Armagnac by Charles Neal
Grands Crus of Bordeaux by Hans Walraven
Sauternes by Jeffrey Benson and Alastair McKenzie
Africa Uncorked by John and Erica Platter
Chip Cassidy's Wine Travels by Chip Cassidy
Wines of Baja California by Ralph Amey
Ghost Wineries of the Napa Valley by Irene Whitford Haynes
Terroir by James E. Wilson
A Wine Growers Guide by Philip M. Wagner
Northern Wine Works by Thomas A. Plocher
Concepts in Wine Chemistry by Yair Margalit
Concepts in Wine Technology by Yair Margalit
Winery Technology & Operations by Yair Margalit
Understanding Wine Technology by David Bird
Red & White by Max Allen
The Taste of Wine by Emile Peynaud
The Commonsense Book of Wine by Leon D. Adams
The University Wine Course by Marian Baldy
The Global Encyclopedia of Wine Edited by Peter Forrestal
Zinfandel by Cathleen Francisco
Wine Heritage by Dick Rosano
Napa Wine by Charles L. Sullivan
A Century of Wine Edited by Stephen Brook
Sommeliers Guide to Restaurants in America Catherine Fallis and Yves Sauboua
The Bartender's Black Book by Stephen Kittredge Cunningham
The Wine Buyer's Record Book by Ralph Steadman
You're a Real Wine Lover When... by Bert Witt
The Champagne Cookbook by Malcolm R. Hebert
New Adventures in Wine Cookery
Favorite Recipes of California Winemakers
Wine in Everyday Cooking by Patricia Ballard
Wine, Food & the Good Life by Arlene Mueller and Dorothy Indelicato
Fine Wine in Food by Patricia Ballard
Wine Lovers Cookbook Malcolm R. Hebert
The French Paradox by Gene Ford
The Science of Healthy Drinking by Gene Ford

WINE INVESTMENT
for
PORTFOLIO
DIVERSIFICATION

*How Collecting Fine Wines
Can Yield Greater Returns
than Stocks and Bonds*

MAHESH KUMAR

BA(HONS), ACMA, ATT, CMC, MBA, DIPIC

FOREWORD BY MICHAEL BROADBENT

THE WINE APPRECIATION GUILD
SAN FRANCISCO

Wine Investment for Portfolio Diversification:
How Collecting Fine Wines can Yield Greater Returns than Stocks and Bonds

The Wine Appreciation Guild
360 Swift Avenue
South San Francisco CA 94080
(650) 866-3020
www.wineappreciation.com

Author: Mahesh Kumar
Editors: Bryan Imelli, Maurice T. Sullivan
Graphic Design and Typesetting: Diane Spencer Hume

ISBN: 1-891267-84-1

Library of Congress Control Number: 2004094947

Printed in the United States of America

To My Mum & Dad,
My Beloved Wife Sasha
& My New Baby Boy Roman-Boston

CONTENTS

References

Bibliography

Index

NOTATIONS

Notations differ widely in literatures. To make the reading experience more congenial, I've listed below all the symbols used in this book:

b:	Beta
CAPM:	Capital Asset Pricing Model
CML:	Capital Markets Line
COVAR:	Covariance
DB:	Diversification Benefit
DJIA:	Dow Jones Industrial Average
EF:	Efficient Frontier
ER:	Expected Return
ERFW:	Expected Return on Fine Wine 50 Index
ERFT/DJ:	Expected Return on FTSE 100 Index/Dow Jones Index
ERM:	Exchange Rate Mechanism
FW50:	Fine Wine 50 Index
FTGB:	FT Government Bonds Index
FTSE 100:	FTSE 100 Index
FTSE 100(IR):	FTSE 100 Index with Income Reinvested
LIBOR:	London Inter-bank Offer Rate
RFr:	Risk Free Rate
RG:	Risk Grade
RGp:	Portfolio Diversified Risk Grade
RI:	Risk Impact
% RI:	Percentage Risk Impact

SML: Security Markets Line

SD ors: Standard Deviation

TL: Transformation Line

URGp: Portfolio Un-diversified Risk Grade

USGB: US 30-Year Treasury Bonds Index

VAR: Variance

FOREWORD
MICHAEL BROADBENT

No question: wine is a commodity, albeit consumable and, at its best, the most civilized of beverages. As long as wine has been made, which takes us back into the mists of time, it has been traded in; records exist from the Middle East, "the cradle of the vine," ancient Greece and Egypt of the Pharaohs. They advise the best time to ship—for example, overnight from the Greek Islands to Alexandria, using specially designed "speed" galleys to avoid the heat of the day. Later the Phoenicians were the major traders, followed by the conquering Romans who, well beyond their shores, were propagators and producers. These ancients knew the importance of climate and weather conditions, as well as the suitability of vineyard sites. Thus, long ago, the importance of vintages and the quality—and style—of wine was firmly established, hand in hand with the concept of value and price and the laws of supply and demand.

In the Middle Ages, the consumption of wine was colossal; indeed, with wool, it was the most important commodity traded on the English market. Rich London wine merchants were regular moneylenders to the reigning monarch. However, until the introduction in the 18th century of bottles with corks, and the ability to store wine, virtually all wine was consumed within the year of its production, so the concept of investment as we know it today did not exist.

There is nothing new about speculation, though specific records are hard to come by; that is, anything predating the 18th century. Happily, Christie's unique wine auction archives, which house every auctioneer's catalog from James Christie's first sale in 1766 (including quantities of "fine claret" and "fine old Maderia (sic)'), provide interesting information. In the 18th century the one wine that was renowned for its ability to improve with age was madeira; not in a bottle and "laid down" in a traditional English—or Scottish—cellar, but in a cask. At that time the madeira trade was enormous by any standards, thanks to almost limitless consumption not only in the British Isles but throughout the colonies, for it was the only type of wine able to survive the heat and humidity of the Carolinas, Georgia, the subtropical West Indies, India and the tropical East. British merchantmen picked up "pipes" of madeira in Funchal en route to the Indies and it was soon discovered that the heat and rolling of the barrels in the hold of the ship resulted in a marked improvement of flavor. The importation of wine that had benefited from a return voyage, better still a lengthy sojourn in the Indies, found a ready market in the home country. The much-traveled wine had not only improved in taste but greatly in price.

The second half of the 18th century abounded with examples of speculative enterprise, almost all relating to madeira. Christies, in September 1790, listed thirty pipes "much improved by its continuance in India," which averaged 40 each; and the following month "39 pipes of most excellent London Particular Madeira which has been to the Brazils;" and in May 1791 "Seventeen pipes…the Property of an East India Captain…the Quality and Flavor of the First Sort having by Duration in India been greatly ameliorated by the Climate!"

Amongst the first of James Christie's auctions of wine was "A pipe of very fine old high flavoured Madeira, neat as imported" and sold, on January 25, 1768, on behalf of Josias Dupré Esq. who "returned from the West Indies on being appointed Governor of Madras." The following September Christie's sold "a catalogue of Neat Wines, property of Captain Fletcher from the West Indies."

A century later there was an example of unwise speculation in an otherwise excellent vintage. At Christie's in June 1874 there was a two-day auction of "3400 dozens of Claret of the Vintage 1865, being a portion of the stock of that Vintage, the Property of Messrs Todd-

Heatley & Co., the Whole were Bottled at their Cellars in the Adelphi in the autumn of 1868, where they still remain." Quite clearly, the firm had bought at the top of the market and was obliged to unload after the Bordeaux market collapsed. Well over half failed to reach their reserves. And the wine—all top class names: Chateau Margaux (150 dozen), Lafite (47 dozen), and Palmer (285 dozen!), plus Cos, Giscours, Leoville and others. Most of all the foregoing sold in the 38 to 60 shillings per dozen range; 41 dozen Kirwan failed to find a buyer (a wonderful wine incidentally. I first tasted it in 1970, one hundred and five years after the vintage).

In the last two decades of the 19th century, indeed until World War I, Bordeaux was in the doldrums. The 1920s were boom times, with the price of Lafite 1929 reaching an all-time high. Those who bought speculatively at these prices regretted it, for euphoria was followed by the world recession.

After World War II, the main problem was for Bordeaux to get production and trade back on its feet, and for the traditional British merchants to replenish stocks. Vines were replanted and, in the 1950s, the chais renovated. However, capital was short and prices still uneconomically low. Growing demand and the reentry of the American market went hand in hand with the high inflation, resulting in overheating. For example, the opening price for Chateau Lafite 1959 was 11,000 francs per tonneau (4 hogsheads, 96 dozen bottles) whereas the opening price for the 1969, a much poorer vintage, had increased to 70,000 francs per tonneau. After 1969 the market got completely out of hand and Bordeaux prices escalated. Buyers were frantic. The outrageous asking prices for the poor 1972 vintage (together with the oil crisis) triggered the collapse. For over two years cash dried up; in Bordeaux no wine was bought or sold. In the mid 1970s the trade started to unload. Those with cash in hand, who bought at the mammoth Christie's trade sales in 1975 and 1976 (for Calvet, Cordier and Delor in Bordeaux, and for Bass Charrington in London) made a fortune when they resold when the markets recovered. To give an example, 2,000 dozen bottles of 1970 Mouton-Rothschild belonging to

Bass Charrington sold for an average price of 74 per dozen (ex Mouton's cellars). One buyer who paid 54 per dozen for a 100-dozen lot sold at Christie's, all 100 dozen, at 990 per dozen only a handful of years later.

Christie's first published an index of wine auction prices, listed by chateau, in 1972. Later, Christie's Price Index included a "comparative price chart." It made interesting reading. For example, the 1959 Lafite mentioned earlier, in 1974, the lowest point of the wine recession, sold for only 100 per dozen bottles; by 1985 it had reached 2,100. But, of huge significance, as editor, I added to the chart the "United Kingdom index of consumer goods and services." In 1974 the UK index was "100," by 1985, "323" and only three years later "422." Now of course it is out of sight. On the other hand, we are currently going through a period of low inflation and low interest rates.

That said: is wine a wise investment or bold speculation? It's a fine dividing line.

My advice is to buy the wines you particularly like, of good vintages only—and with your own money—and look forward to enjoying them when mature. With luck and good management you might have the additional benefit of reselling the stock surplus of your drinking requirements at a price that reflects its enhanced quality and diminished availability.

No need to rely solely on luck. A serious study of Mahesh Kumar's structured analysis could be of considerable help.

—Michael Broadbent

AUTHOR'S PREFACE

This book sets out to answer the following four questions. Firstly, does holding a portfolio of Fine Wine as part of a diversified portfolio of equities and government bonds increase portfolio expected return and reduce portfolio risk? Secondly, what are the optimal weights of Fine Wine, equities and government bonds in the asset allocation decision? Thirdly, what is the extent of the diversification benefits from investing in Fine Wine? And fourthly, how risky is investing in Fine Wine?

To answer these four questions in a logical way, this book is divided into seven chapters. Chapter One provides some background information on Fine Wine investment. Chapter Two reviews literature on the performance of collectibles and Fine Wine. Chapter Three reviews Modern Portfolio Theory (MPT), portfolio diversification and the Capital Asset Pricing Model (CAPM). Chapter Four provides an overview of the methodology used and rationale adopted. Chapter Five critically evaluates and interprets the results. Chapter Six calculates and evaluates the risks associated with investing in Fine Wine. Chapter Seven summarises the concepts discussed in the previous chapter, presents the conclusions of the study and raises some additional alternative investment issues.

The international Fine Wine market has experienced considerable change in the past decade with increased interest from sophisticated industry investors and heightened consumer demand. This change has triggered the sharp expansion in global demand for Fine Wines. For the purposes of this study, Fine Wine is defined as the most acknowledged and prestigious blue chip, exclusively French red wine produced by Châteaux from the Bordeaux region of France, which commands a global consumer and investment following that provides an established marketability. Some wines from other parts of France, particularly Burgundy and the Rhone Valley, along with wines from other areas of the world, for example California, can also provide profitable investment opportunities. There is, nonetheless, a far greater amount of data and literature on Bordeaux wines and its investment potential then there are for these other wines and regions.

There is currently little academic literature on Fine Wine investment, although both academia and the commercial world have produced reviews and studies on Fine Wine appreciation and its pricing. Different, often opposing, claims have been made with regard to Fine Wine investment. Traditional diversification involves holding international financial assets. This book addresses the opportunities of diversifying into non-traditional financial assets, for example collectibles such as art, but with a much greater emphasis on Fine Wine; and by using portfolio theory, it determines and quantifies the diversification benefits of investing in Fine Wine and establishes the effects on expected return and the risk of holding Fine Wine as part of a well-diversified portfolio of traditional financial assets, notably equities and bonds. The results demonstrate that a Fine Wine portfolio can be a profitable investment as part of a diversified portfolio of traditional financial assets, thereby increasing the portfolio expected return and reducing portfolio risk. The major determinants of a good investment have been identified, and strong evidence supporting investment activity in Fine Wine has been found and documented.

This study has a UK and US investor focus only, but it is possible to widen the scope to international investors, using international indices. The methodology may be repeated using different indices for Fine Wine and equities,[1] or repeated using other non-financial assets or collectibles such as fine art or antiques.

Stock markets that once seemed to know only a single direction—straight up—continue to stagger even after the 40% losses seen in the past few years. Amid all the upheaval in financial markets, even market strategists and economists complain that the markets lack compelling themes. Smart investors tend to be those who recognize large shifts in the economy early on and invest for the long-term. In the 70s, gold investors thrived; in the 80s it was the real estate owner's turn. In the 90s the action shifted to stocks. And what will this decade bring? Alternative investments (Fine Wine, Fine Art or Antiques) will make a breakthrough and compensate investors for their disappointing equity, bond and cash portfolio returns. Without the double-digit investment gains that were common in the 80s and 90s, investors may either have to save more or get wiser and wake up to the world of alternative investments if they want to end up with the same amount of money down the road.

"It is not the facts that decide; people have to choose between imperfect alternatives on the basis of uncertain knowledge and fragmentary understanding" (Beatty, 1998).[2] Peter Drucker's comment about business decisions can equally apply to decisions about Fine Wine. From an economic viewpoint the Fine Wine market is an example of laissez faire capitalism, one where supply tends to stimulate demand and the commodity tends to become more highly valued as their original purpose is lost.

Historically, a wine's lack of price volatility compared to the stock market has been one of its major attractions. The Fine Wine market tends to be less volatile than financial markets, and is less susceptible to market downturns and adverse economic conditions; only global recession tends to significantly affect wine prices. High prices for wine can often generate demand rather than act as a deterrent. But, as with everything else, Fine Wine prices can fall as well as rise. Still, Fine Wine has proven to be an effective hedge against recession, inflation and financial assets.

I'm not suggesting holding Fine Wine as a single investment alternative to either equities or bonds, but simply holding Fine Wine as part of a well-diversified portfolio, thereby potentially achieving greater diversification benefits.

This study is based on Modern Portfolio Theory and portfolio diversification. Harry Markowitz (1952),[3] the 1990 Nobel Prize winner in Economic Sciences, pioneered the portfolio selection model, which is premised on the mean-variance model that is dependent upon variables such as expected return, standard deviations (risk) and correlations between asset returns. The theory arises from the recognition that risks exist and this creates different expected returns associated with diversified investment.

In the traditional Markowitz model, the investor maximizes returns subject to a volatility constraint. Further work undertaken by William Sharpe (1963)[4] states that investors seek to achieve the best possible trade-off between risk and return. Diversification reduces both the upside and downside potential and allows for more consistent performance under a wide range of economic conditions. The CAPM provides investors with a precise prediction of the relationship between an asset's risk and expected return, providing a benchmark return for evaluating alternative investments.[5]

Modern Portfolio Theory relies on a static, fixed time horizon in which investors are not required to adjust their investment decisions. Nonetheless, in practice, investment objectives, funding priorities and liquidity needs may change. The inputs are not constant and the outputs are sensitive to changes in the expected return and volatility of expected returns. Estimating with a high degree of accuracy the expected return and correlations upon which the entire optimization exercise relies is critical.

This study outlines the key concepts of portfolio theory and the optimal asset allocation decision, with a greater emphasis on portfolio diversification. For the purposes of statistical analysis a Fine Wine Index has been created made up of 50 investment grade Fine Wines.[6] The monthly returns for this Fine Wine 50 Index have been compared with those of leading (1) UK financial indices; FTSE 100 Index, and the FT Government Bonds Index (commonly referred in the financial markets as the FT Government All Stocks Index) and (2) US financial indices; Dow Jones Industrial Average, and the US 30 Year Treasury Bonds Index, in rolling 5-year time spans for the 20 and 21 year periods from 1983 to 2002 and 1983 to 2003, inclusive.

The results also demonstrate that the (1) Fine Wine 50 Index and the FTSE 100 Index and (2) Fine Wine 50 Index and the Dow Jones Index are uncorrelated: the Fine Wine 50 Index does not track the FTSE 100 Index or the Dow Jones Index and thus brings about significant diversification benefits. Furthermore, portfolios consisting of Fine Wine have a higher expected return per unit of risk. Investing in the Fine Wine 50 Index, when historic returns on the Fine Wine 50 Index have been higher than CAPM expected returns, gives an average return greater than its contribution to risk of overall portfolio of assets. In absolute risk terms, holding Fine Wine is less volatile than equities for a given return.

It is important to note that his book does not attempt to arrive at an ideal portfolio consisting of specific weights of Fine Wine, equities and government bonds. The results suggest that there are higher expected returns when investing in a diversified portfolio consisting of Fine Wine and equities, rather than a portfolio comprising of just equities and government bonds.

Superior returns are achieved when portfolios consist of both the Fine Wine 50 Index and the FTSE 100 Index, and the Fine Wine 50 Index and the Dow Jones Index. Over relatively short time horizons the results suggest that a portfolio consisting of Fine Wine and equities will outperform one solely dominated by equities without a significant increase in volatility. Over the long-term this trend becomes more obvious.

This book also does not attempt to deny that in some periods the risk free asset (3-month LIBOR or the 3-month Euro/Dollar Deposit Rate), or the FTSE 100 Index, or the Dow Jones Index achieve returns that are superior to and less volatile than an investment in the Fine Wine 50 Index. Nonetheless, the investment potential of Fine Wine in this work, and especially the 10 year period from 1993 to 2002, is not consistent with the findings of some previous academic studies, which claim that wine does not compare favorably to traditional financial assets. The results demonstrate with robust empirical evidence that Fine Wine does compare favorably with traditional financial assets. But economists will no doubt claim that any desirable characteristics of Fine Wine are capitalized into their prices.

The dramatic rise in Fine Wine prices in the early 1980s and in the 1990s (since the 1982 vintage) suggests the possible presence of a rational bubble. Fine Wine investors, like those who invest in common stocks, may believe that prices have pressed ahead to unsustainable levels but continue to buy in the belief that short-term prospects for continued gains are sufficient to compensate for the risk that the price bubble might burst. The pattern of positive correlations for short horizons and low or negative correlations for longer horizons is consistent with bubble like behaviour, as shown with Cutler et al. (1991)[7] in their review of international evidence in the market for equities, bonds, foreign exchange and various real assets.

Maintaining a diversified portfolio of blue chip wine minimizes the risk of over-exposure to a specific wine. Returns may be enhanced by the application of a simple but effective portfolio management methodology; a 'relative value analysis' approach may be able to select wines and/or vintages that are under or over-valued. After extensive and detailed research of the Global Financial, Bordeaux and Fine Wine markets, both in current and historical terms, I'm certain that these market trends will continue. As a result, the international demand for Fine Wine will advance whilst the supply of existing vintages is ever decreasing and new production remains fairly static. In other words, Fine Wine presents an outstanding investment opportunity and should merit serious consideration by professional and private investors. The international Fine Wine secondary market currently has an annual turnover in excess of US$1 billion.[8] Having started from a traditionally fragmented and somewhat unsophisticated position, it is now developing into an increasingly professional marketplace, continuously attracting new consumers and investors. Fine Wine prices have historically and consistently outperformed leading international financial indices such as the FTSE 100 Index and the Dow Jones Index, as demonstrated in this study. Due to the envisaged future supply and demand situation, Fine Wine prices will continue to outperform leading international financial markets. Based on the empirical evidence, holding Fine Wine as part of a diversified portfolio of traditional financial assets, namely equities and bonds, enhances portfolio expected return and brings about significant diversification benefits.

ENDNOTES

1. *Decanter Magazine,* Bordeaux Index (consists of approximately 1300 wines, not all investment grade), FTSE All Share (more representative of the market) or S&P 500 (international perspective).
2. Beatty, J., *The World According to Drucker,* Orion Business, London, 1st Edition, 1998.
3. Markowitz, H., "Portfolio Selection," *Journal of Finance,* March, 1952.
4. Sharpe, W., "A Simplified Model of Portfolio Analysis," *Management Science,* January, 1963.
5. Sharpe, W., "Capital Asset Prices: A Theory of Market Equilibrium," *Journal of Finance,* September, 1964; Linter, J., "The Valuation of Risky Assets and the Selection of Risky Investments in Stock Portfolios and Capital Budgets," *Review of Economics and Statistics,* February, 1965; Mossin, J., "Equilibrium in a Capital Asset Market," *Econometrica,* October, 1966.
6. *See Appendix 2.*
7. Cutler, D.M., Poterba, J.M., & Summers, L.M., "Speculative Dynamics," *Review of Economic Studies,* 58:3, 1991, pp. 529–46.
8. Fine Wine Management Company.

FROM THE PUBLISHER

In the short months leading up to the publication of this book, partaking in an ancient and informal custom in book production, I polled friends and colleagues on the work's topic to gauge its potential reception by the reading public. I wasn't surprised by the opinions of people in the wine business who are directly compensated by the practice of laying wine down. But what surprised me was the general anti-wine-investor vehemence of wine writers, journalists, critics and the like. They were outraged at the thought of someone collecting wine with any intention of profit. After all, wine is a "means to pleasure and good living," right? But discerning wine critics and writers understand the multiple benefits of investing in wine.

Below is an excerpt from *Collectors versus Consumers* written by Robert M. Parker, Jr., and published in his 6th Edition *Wine Buyer's Guide*, included here by his permission.

"The third type of collector, the investor, is motivated by the possibility of reselling the wines for profit. Eventually, most or all of these wines return to the marketplace, and much of it wends its way into the hands of serious consumers who share it with their spouses or good friends. Of course, they often must pay dearly for the privilege, but wine is not the only product that falls prey to such manipulation. I hate to think of wine being thought of primarily as an investment, but the world's finest wines do appreciate significantly in value, and it would be foolish to ignore the fact that more and more shrewd investors are looking at wine as a way of making money."

Making sound wine investment choices is not much different than investing in a fine home, a classic automobile, antiques or art: All possessions, when selected wisely, may greatly increase in value over time and give immense pleasure to the owner. I revel in the experience of opening a 25-year old Bordeaux at a family holiday or special occasion; I know that I would not pay today's price for the pleasure, but this too is reaping the rewards of fine wine investment. The same can be said for the anticipatory joy of putting away a very good case of Port at your son's birth, knowing that, when the times comes, he can sell it at a greatly increased value or drink it. And as anyone who has shared the experience knows, it's quite a buzz eyeing those rare old bottles in my cellar, anticipating their hidden pleasures and relaxing in the commodious sense of security that no matter what goes wrong in this world, at least I will be drinking well.

The scorn of most wine critics seems hardly fair. No wine-loving wine investor looks at wine "primarily as an investment"; that it can be an investment is an attendant benefit. If you can sell off your last few bottles of appreciated Yquem for a profit what's the harm? Some wine critic might respond to this by saying, "how can a sincere wine-lover sell off his last bottles of Yquem?" To him I say, " at 750% its original price, that's how."

A few myths need to be cast out. Of most alternative investments (fine-art, collectibles), wine is not only the most fiscally prudent it's the most *fiscally accessible*. This seems intuitively baffling to a lot of people, but it's a misnomer to call wine investment "elitist." The affectation surrounding wine appreciation helps christen it as such, and as a general rule people are scared off by things that make them feel like a rube, but after doing the numbers it all makes sense. The same amount of money an average worker puts into his 401K could buy him several cases of first growth Bordeaux. For most middle-income portfolios, an investment of this size could bring a substantial diversification. He should of course only do this after taking sound advice and self-educating. Reading this book is a good start.

Elliott Mackey, Publisher

ACKNOWLEDGEMENTS

I would like to thank my publisher, Elliott Mackey, for his commitment to this study from inception to completion. His advice in making this book a first of its kind and the fine-tuning of its contents have been invaluable.

I would like to thank George Clowes from Fine Wine Management Limited for his valuable contribution throughout this study. His encouragement and generosity in supplying me with financial data and sharing his own personal experiences and contacts have been second to none.

Finally, I would like to thank my beloved wife, Sasha, for her encouragement, patience and significant contribution to the making of this book.

INTRODUCTION TO
FINE WINE INVESTMENT

FINE WINE INVESTMENT

lthough other areas in the world are producing investment grade wine, this book defines Fine Wine as blue chip, exclusively French red wine produced by Châteaux from the Bordeaux region of France. This is because the area is highly regarded for its historical and consistent production of Fine Wine of exceptional quality. Selected red wines from Bordeaux are universally regarded as the best-in-class Fine Wines. Consequently this Fine Wine commands a worldwide consumer and investment following providing a ready marketability. In Bordeaux there are 115,000 hectares under vine, 113,000 of which produce appellation controlee wine. The average age of the vines under production is some 25 years. There are approximately 13,000 winegrowers, 400 shippers, of which the largest account for 90% of the total turnover, and 150 wine brokers.

Though there were many individual attempts in the 18th and early 19th century to class Bordeaux wine, it was not until 1855 that France officially adopted a Fine Wine Index classifying the wines of the Medoc (plus Haut Brion) from First Growth to Fifth Growth based on quality and price. There are now 5 producers who are classified as First Growth, 14 as Second Growth, 14 as Third Growth, 10 as Fourth

Growth and 18 as Fifth Growth. Whilst the classifications of 1855 have hardly been changed since inception they have held up remarkably well. Nonetheless, there are certain Bordeaux producers of Fine Wines regarded by the marketplace as ranking alongside those of higher classifications. Château Lynch-Bages, classified Fifth Growth, trades alongside Second Growths; and unclassified wines from the Pomerol region in France, most notably Château Petrus, are trading well ahead of First Growths. Another example is Château Cheval Blanc, which also trades on par with First Growths.

Prices for Fine Wine can vary from as little as £200 per case (12 x 75cl bottles) to as high as £20,000 per case and sometimes more.[1] Fine Wine from Bordeaux would always make the majority of any investment portfolio. Nonetheless, there are certain wines from other parts of France, particularly Burgundy and the Rhone Valley, along with certain wines from other areas of the world, for instance the US and Australia, that can provide investment opportunities from time to time, and merit investment consideration. Champagne should rarely be regarded as an investment opportunity with the exception of certain vintage years primarily because producers hold excessive stocks of approximately 85 million cases, 3 years worldwide consumption.[2]

The Fine Wine market has shifted from an emerging market in the 1980s to an established investment market in the 1990s. Traditionally, the Fine Wine market has been somewhat non-commercial often ruled by emotion rather than being entirely profit driven. The traditional approach was one of "buy two, drink one free." Historically it has been possible to effectively drink free by buying the wine in the primary market (en primeur) or in the secondary market at the beginning of a Fine Wine's life, holding the wine until it becomes drinkable and then selling part of the investment in order to reduce the book cost to zero.

Recently the Fine Wine market has seen the emergence of new consumers and now attracts the attention of sophisticated international investors who have come to appreciate that the structure of the market and the commodity involved provides opportunities for the realization of above average financial returns. Whilst the "buy two, drink one free" strategy will continue, increasingly Fine Wine is being regarded as a pure investment medium with the professional and private investor having no intention of ever consuming any of the investment.

Western Europe continues to dominate the global wine market with the UK providing the second largest market to France. North America continues to reflect their preference for more expensive wines currently accounting for 15% of worldwide sales but only 8% of volume.[3] While the developing market consumers are increasing their consumption of red wine from Bordeaux, they are tending towards quality rather than quantity. Nonetheless the main engines of future growth lie outside the traditional markets of Western Europe and North America. The educational process of the developing market consumer is very much in its early days. The emerging economies of Eastern Europe and Latin America are anticipated to demonstrate significant growth in consumption. The strongest growth region is predicted to be Eastern Europe expecting to be on level par with North America in terms of total market share.

In the Far East and other developing markets, higher priced red wines from Bordeaux are becoming prized as a measure of status and wealth coupled with the heightening perception as to the health benefits of consumption. A noticeable snob value is becoming attached to being seen drinking Fine Wine. To this end Fine Wine continues to experience rising demand. It is expected that Fine Wine will increasingly command a status-related following amongst developing-market consumers. The profile of developing-market wine buyers is primarily that of a consumer as opposed to one of an investor. In more developed markets professional and private investors are increasingly investing in Fine wine, which naturally creates demand for investment grade wines from Bordeaux.

The demand for Fine Wine within the hotels, restaurants and catering sectors has shown rapid and sustained growth over the past decade in line with the consumer's heightened awareness of the wide variety of available wines coupled with a heightened appreciation as to the quality of these wines. Hoteliers, restaurateurs and caterers have a growing recognition that a varied and comprehensive selection of wine constitutes an increasingly important contribution to customer appeal and consequent bigger profits.

A Brief History of the Bordeaux Wine Market

The discovery of a new type of vine resistant to harsh winters changed the course of viticulture history during the 1st century AD. The Biturica, this new grape variety, was planted in the vineyards of the Rich Biturigians, the first settlers of Bordeaux.

In 1152 Eleanor, Duchess of Aquitaine, married Henry Plantagenet, future King of England. There started a thriving trade between Aquitaine and the British Isles. Twice a year a fleet left England to 'fetch the wine' whilst simultaneously exporting food, textiles and metals to Bordeaux. This trade came to an abrupt end in 1453 when the French won the Battle of Castillon and took back Aquitaine.

In the 17th century the Bordeaux region saw the appearance of new customers such as the Dutch, Hanseats and Bretons. This change in the wine market coincided with a profound change in the nature of the wine itself. The 18th century growth in Bordeaux wine exports came from Santo Domingo and the Lesser Antilles, and as a result of this colonial trade Bordeaux experienced great prosperity up until the French Revolution. At this time England accounted for only 10% of all wine exports although Fine Wines were very much sought after by London's high society who considered wine fashionable. The general situation at the beginning of the 19th century in the Gironde vineyards was one of commercial weariness. In the mid 1800s the devastating vine disease, Oidium, struck the vineyards and it was not until 1857 that sulphur treatments were found to get rid of the disease. Once the hazards of Oidium were under control the Bordeaux vineyards entered an era of prosperity triggered by a quartet of superb vintages: 1844, 1846, 1847 and 1848. Furthermore, at this time the famous 1855 Classification was made of some of Gironde's most famous Châteaux including those from the Medoc, Sauternes and Haut-Brion in the Graves.

This prosperity peaked with the 1864 and 1865 vintages. Production and exports increased phenomenally with England proving to be Bordeaux's best market both in volume and quality. However, from 1879 to 1892 Bordeaux faced what proved to be a near devastating crisis in the form of a small yellow insect, Phylloxera, with a taste for vine root. The market recovered slightly with the great 1893 vintage (similar to the 2003). The grafting of French grape varieties onto American rootstock fortunately remedied this, but brought with it attendant difficulties; this migrant rootstock introduced mildew. The mildew was finally brought under control by 'bouillie bordelaise,' a mixture of lime and copper sulphate.

At the turn of the century, rampant fraud and a huge drop in prices posed a new crisis for Bordeaux. This led to the introduction of the new French wine laws in 1911 that prohibited the use of the name 'Bordeaux' on wine from anywhere outside the Gironde. The legal boundaries were further defined in 1936 with the formation of the Institut National des Appellations d'Origine adding quality control to that of geographical origin. New classifications were made in Graves and Saint Emilion in 1955 and after recovering from the disastrous frost of 1956 demand from around the world coupled with commercial acumen resulted in the current and continuing period of prosperity.[4]

MARKETING AND DISTRIBUTION
IN THE BORDEAUX WINE MARKET

The Conseil Interprofessionnel du Vin de Bordeaux (the Bordeaux Wine Council) conduct a marketing campaign from September through to the following August every year that promotes wine from the new vintage as well as stocks held by Châteaux and Negociants.[5] Châteaux on average carry stocks of all past vintages equivalent in total to only about 1 year's current production, while Negociants stock an average of 6 months worth of sales. This means that even if the harvest fails the marketplace remains supplied, to some extent, by stocks.[6]

Each March the world wine trade descends on Bordeaux to taste the wines produced from the harvest of the previous September. Whilst the wines are in their infancy they are tasted from the barrel and firm opinions are formed as to the quality and future potential of these wines. The world's wine trade and press then publish their findings and these opinions determine the initial demand and consequent opening price levels of the new wines.[7]

That said, the Fine Wines produced by the First Growth Châteaux, the majority of Second Growth Châteaux along with selected other producers including some of those from the Pomerol region will always command a premium price compared to those wines from Châteaux which are perceived to produce wines of lesser quality and consistency.

In the course of April and May after the world's wine trade has formulated their opinions the Châteaux commence sales of their previous year's production. They instruct the Courtiers[8] to begin testing the marketplace by means of talking to the Negociants. These Negociants will indicate at what price levels they are prepared to buy and the Courtiers under instruction from their clients will then offer stock to the Negociants.

Price levels and volumes sold vary from Château to Château, rates being reliant upon the individual Château's financial and tax positions. Generally, Châteaux tend not to retain any significant volume of production for any length of time.

The Negociants then deal directly with the world's wine trade frequently achieving substantial profit margins. This initial trade of the new wines is known as buying 'En Primeur'. These Fine Wines are effectively sold as wine futures. In the US En Primeur sales are referred to as 'futures' as they will not be bottled until the September of the following year and will then only start being shipped in the spring of the next year. This means that a wine produced from the harvest of September 2000 will only be delivered in the spring of the year 2003. Once sold by the Negociants these new wine futures enter the secondary market and do on occasion trade a number of times before shipment.

This marketing and distribution method of the Châteaux is a time honoured, if somewhat archaic, system. It has existed in its current form for generations and is difficult to thwart. However in certain exceptional instances it is possible for international brokers or even individual investors to deal directly with the Châteaux and it is envisaged that this will gradually become more commonplace. Certain Châteaux are becoming increasingly aware of the benefits of becoming actively involved in the marketing of their own production.[9]

For all top producers, not only is the vineyard a limited defined area, yields are deliberately kept low in order to achieve the very best quality of Fine Wine. Châteaux are increasingly declassifying a significant part of their crop in order to ensure that only the best grapes are used in the production of their flagship Fine Wines. The remaining grapes are used to produce their unclassified second label wines.

Fine Wine Investment Today

Different, often opposing, claims have been made with regards to Fine Wine investment performance. Some writers claim that Fine Wine has consistently outperformed all other forms of recognised investments and is unaffected by recession, interest rate changes, and stock market fluctuations.[10] Despite it being difficult to make a precise distinction between the investor and collector, one is certain of the fact that the number of people who buy Fine Wine as an investment has increased significantly over the past decade and continues to attract new investors to the market.

The primary objective of wine investment is to make a profit on its disposal, one that is greater than the disposal of an equivalent risky investment or equivalent monetary investment. Understanding Fine Wine as an investment is as simple as understanding the market forces of supply and demand. Fine Wine is produced in strict finite quantities. Thus heightened global demand drives up the value of the wine that remains in the market. This brings about the desired pre-conditions for investment in wine and creates the basis for a stable market. Many investors buy Fine Wine when first released, taking advantage of "en primeur"[11] prices. The Fine Wine investment market created a new generation of investors and traders in the 1990s. The market has become more sophisticated, offering greater opportunities to buy and sell wine. Trading has become more proactive and speculative. Brokers offer advice on what and when to buy and sell as well as constructing and managing portfolios.

The name Bordeaux is synonymous with wine investment. Red Bordeaux wine has an established resale history and is the primary investment medium. It remains the leading investment grade wine for auction prices. The value of Bordeaux wine is more readily identifiable, the 1855 classification providing a framework for evaluating wine most widely held and traded.

Investment grade wine can have a life span of up to 50 years. There is a sharp rise for 6 to 18 months following the release of the wine, and in the lesser years, prices can fall during this period. The value then stabilizes, or rises at a slower rate, until the wine becomes ready to consume, normally after 15 to 20 years. After this period, stocks start to diminish and prices start to rise once more. The wine then continues to mature and prices rise until the end of its life.

Investment in Fine Wine entails buying the best vintages of blue chip Châteaux when first released. Wooden cases holding 12 bottles are the basic trading unit in the Fine Wine trade. Nonetheless, there may be occasions when it is imprudent to invest in some Fine Wines at an early stage. This is because the vintage is disappointing and/or the opening en primeur prices are considered too high and expected to offer more reasonable value at a later date in the secondary market.

There are 3 optimum times to sell Fine Wines depending on the investor's investment horizon: buying early en primeur and then selling 18 months later; holding onto the wine until it is at peak maturity and then selling when the prices have notably reached their optimum price levels; or other Fine Wines offer greater potential for percentage price appreciation. Research has shown that only 3 or 4 vintages out of every 10 years are of a high enough quality to be used as investment wines.[12] (A good vintage is considered to be one that experienced optimal climate conditions for a specific grape variety.) Depending upon the harvest and the various qualities of the wine produced, different vintages and wines will reach their maturity at varying times. Some wines will need to be consumed within 5 years of production whilst others will last for up to 100 years significantly increasing the potential for investment.

THE PRIMARY MARKET: *EN PRIMEUR*

The primary market is led by Bordeaux Negociants offering stocks of Fine Wine at the beginning of the wine's life. Thus, the simplest and most attractive method of acquiring wine is buying en primeur, or wine futures; that is, buying wine when it is still in the barrel. This in theory offers the greatest potential for higher returns. Fundamentally the Negociants are selling a Fine Wine future as the wine is still in the barrel and will not be bottled and shipped for some 3 years. These Fine Wine futures then trade readily in the secondary market. The key markets for *en primeur* sales are North America 20%, Germany 15%, Switzerland 15%, UK 15%, France 10%, Belgium 10% and the rest of the world 15%.[13]

Historically, buying *en primeur* has proved to be the optimum method for securing Fine Wine where one can be assured of impeccable provenance and consequent guaranteed condition. More recently the attention is turning to purchasing and investing in Fine Wines at an early stage.

The attraction to investors is securing sought-after wines at prices lower than subsequent market prices before the wine is bottled. Buying *en primeur* offers an opportunity to buy wine that may not be readily available, except at a premium, because of limited quantities. Château owners benefit from the big increase in futures contracts by locking into high prices and selling 80% of their annual production in one go, very much like an Initial Public Offering. Château owners get paid in advance for that 80% long before the wine is bottled and shipped.[14] Buying wine futures of the finest wines and best vintages makes economic sense, presupposing that investors know early on which years are great and which wines are best.

Buying wine *en primeur* encourages speculation. The greatest disadvantage for the investor is the risk attached to buying an unfinished product. Selling in the intervening period can be problematic since there is no way of determining the market price for a particular wine whilst still in its barrel. In periods of economic recession, prices may fall and there is a greater risk that one of the commercial concerns in the supply chain will fail, leaving investors without any prospect of receiving what they've paid for. Wine futures, unlike commodity futures, are contracts that are not sold on an organised exchange, are not regulated, and cannot be bought on margin.

THE SECONDARY MARKET: AUCTIONS AND ALTERNATIVES

Currently, the secondary market for Fine Wine, centred in the UK, where international investors increasingly store their wine, is estimated to account for a global annual turnover in excess of US$1 billion. A significant part of this trade globally, with the exception of the US, takes place on an "in bond" basis where the Fine Wines do not attract local import duties or taxes until such time as they are removed from bond. The main reasons for any Fine Wine being removed from bond are when it is intended for consumption, retail or to be placed in a private cellar. The US has 52 different sets of regulations, and international and inter-state trading is complex. Duty paid wine has no guaranteed provenance and therefore will trade at a discount to "in bond" wine with a verifiable storage history.

Auction Houses are estimated to account for approximately 12.5% of the global secondary market turnover.[15] Auctions have long been an integral part of the wine trade. Historically, wine auctions were used as a means of selling wine in barrels. Today's commercial auction trade relies on selling bottled wines at all stages of maturity and takes considerable steps to guarantee the wines provenance[16] to protect both the buyer and its own reputation. In auctions, marketing hype and release prices are moved to one side and the market establishes a wine's real value. Price fluctuations reflect the speculative volatility of all commodity markets. Speculative investors weigh up the uncertainties of international exchange rates, vintage reputation and investment horizon. As with all such markets there is a tendency towards instability and fluctuations between boom and bust periods.

Christie's and Sotheby's are the main players in the auctions market. Both Christie's and Sotheby's were founded in the 18th century and are the world's oldest and most prestigious Fine Wine auction houses. Christie's has been auctioning wine since James Christie's first sale in 1766. There were frequent wine sales until the premises were destroyed in World War II. After the war, public auctions of wine were prohibited in England. It was not until Michael Broadbent was appointed head of the new wine department in 1966 that Christie's resumed wine auctions. Both have salesrooms across the globe. Auctions held by Christie's and Sotheby's in London, Paris, Geneva, New York and California provide centralized markets for international wine sellers and buyers to compete freely. Arbitrageurs are well-informed, global operators who produce, market or trade wines in many locations and their position provides good opportunities to take advantage of international price differentials by shifting goods from one market to another.

The trade criticizes auctions for being a relatively expensive place to purchase Fine Wine with no guarantee of provenance unless the wine is "in bond." A detailed comparison of auction prices against a representative cross-section of published trade price-lists indicate that with the 10% buyer's premium, and duty or taxes where applicable, the auction prices tend to be less competitive than those being advertised by the trade.[17] Traditionally, selling Fine Wine at auctions was a relatively long, drawn out affair and sales were as infrequent as once or twice a year. More recently, with the buoyancy and rapid expansion of the Fine Wine market and with greater numbers of collectors or investors chasing fewer blue chip bottles of Fine Wine, not only are prices being driven up, but the turnaround is much more rapid. At auction, prices of Fine Wine are often driven above their 'true value' when demand is rife and where two or more investors are determined to bid for their prized investment. The use of on-line auctions like international internet auctioneer eBay.com has increased trading turnover.[18] Internet wine auctions encourage investor interest and investment activity, increasing the value of wine globally. In addition, the emergence of online auctions have made sought after commodities even more accessible. Nonetheless, the internet is not considered the best medium for the sale and auction of the most prized bottles of Fine Wine because expert advice is not at hand and the wine's provenance, quality and authenticity cannot easily be verified.

There are a significant number of brokers and retailers globally accounting for the vast majority of secondary market turnover. These brokers, whilst they typically enjoy generous margins and offer the most competitive prices, are often constrained by the fact that they are only able to supply a limited amount of stock. Retailers typically concentrate on higher margin bottle and small case lot sales. Nonetheless, there has been a recent emergence of highly professional, competent and well-capitalised specialist Fine Wine brokers who trade on an international basis at competitive margins.

A wine's release price often does not reflect the wine's market worth as perceived by subsequent buyers or investors. There is an apparent mismatch between the sellers and buyers perceptions with regards to market value or price. Appendix 1 shows the price variation of the 1982 Bordeaux First Growths since release.

Investors are able to buy later in the cycle when a wine is closer to maturity and its reputation established in the secondary market. Investors often pay higher prices but benefit from a quicker payback. Alternatively investors can buy stocks in publicly listed wine producing companies. In this case the investor's decision is premised on their understanding of the valuation of the company and its fundamentals.

The next section compares and contrasts blue chip Fine Wine with blue chip stocks and discusses the trading strategies open to Fine Wine investors. Blue chip stocks are widely accepted forms of investment and therefore serve to act as a benchmark when evaluating alternative investments. [19]

TRADING STRATEGIES:
BLUE CHIP FINE WINE VERSUS BLUE CHIP STOCKS

Wine is subject to the law of diminishing returns in that the number of people investing in wines is increasing faster than the number of wines being discovered. The practical problems of investing in wine have much in common with those associated with stocks and shares—the range of choice is enormous and valuations fluctuate continuously. The art in buying wines, as in buying stocks, is to invest in what the financial markets call "neglected value," that is to buy undervalued assets and sell them once the value of these assets have risen to their "fair value." Bull markets are born on pessimism, grow on scepticism and mature on optimism; the best times are to buy at the time of maximum pessimism and sell at the time of maximum optimism. This applies to both Fine Wine and stocks. Fine Wine investors essentially have three options: pay the price, play the market or trade down.

(1) Pay the Price
For some investors the fundamental and intrinsic value of holding blue chip investment grade wine is so great, they will pay the price.

(2) Play the Market or Trade
Playing the market entails taking advantage of market imperfections and temporary situations. Simultaneous price differentials form the basis of arbitrage. Investors can speculate by taking a position in wine futures or identify "sleepers" both in terms of Château and vintage. This "sleepers" strategy entails buying the lesser-classed Châteaux in

great years and the great Châteaux in lesser years. The assumption is that even in a poor year a great vineyard usually produces good wine. In the same way, in the great years lesser vineyards may produce excellent wines—there's a long history of above average returns for Fine Wines produced by Châteaux whose official classification is below that of the quality of the wine that they produce.

(3) Trade Down

Simply buying blue chip investment grade wine tends to drive up its price to a point that no longer presents a good investment. Therefore trading down to pale blue chip wines may present greater investment opportunities. Nonetheless, the difficulty with trading down is the uncertainty of it.

ENDNOTES

1. Fine Wine Management Limited.
2. Champagne Information Bureau & Into Wine (a division of M2 Communications).
3. Bordeaux Index & Euromoniter plc: *Wine: A Wine Survey & Wine Spectator.*
4. Conseil Interprofessionnel Du Vin De Bordeaux (CIVB): The Bordeaux Wine Council.
5. Bordeaux wholesale brokers and stockholders.
6. 1991 was an example of this (CIVB).
7. By far the most influential of the world's wine writers is an American, Robert M. Parker Jr., a lawyer by training who is a widely published author and writes a bi-monthly newsletter, The Wine Advocate. Parker rates each wine on a scale of 50–100 and his judgements have a very significant influence on the demand for and price level of each individual Fine Wine.
8. Independent stock placement agents working for several Châteaux in return for a fixed 2% commission.
9. CIVB.
10. Fine Wine Management Limited, OWC Asset Management, Premier Cru Fine Wine Investment Limited.
11. En Primeur: price of wine when first released while the wine is still in barrel.
12. Fine Wine Management Limited.
13. Wine Spectator & Fine Wine Management Limited.
14. Fuhrman, P., Drinking Your Profits is the Best Revenge, *Forbes*, Vol 145, Issue 13, June, 1990, 3 pages.
15. Christie's & Sotheby's International.
16. Provenance describes a wine's ownership, storage, condition of label and condition of wooden case.
17. Fine Wine Management Limited.
18. O'Riley, M.K., "It's a Cellar's Market," *Director*, January, 2001.
19. OWC Asset Management.

C H A P T E R

2

CRITICAL ANALYSIS OF THE PERFORMANCE OF FINE WINE

THE ALTERNATIVE INVESTMENTS MARKET

Traditional financial investments are no longer delivering the kind of returns investors have been used to. High-yield bonds, hedge funds and private equity funds are too volatile for many investors, who are more conservative in bear markets. Investors are actively searching for alternative investments that are free from many of the risks associated with investing in today's turbulent or underperforming equity markets. Indices tracking the performance of Fine Wine and high-class paintings have held up well in this climate of uncertainty surrounding the global financial markets and low interest rates.[1]

Professors Jianping Mei and Michael Moses (2001),[2] find that Art outperforms fixed income investments but underperforms against equities in the period from 1875 to 2000. Art returns have broadly matched equity returns in the past 50 years. The All Art Index composed by Mei and Moses, based on the resale values of about 4,500 paintings sold at public auction in New York, also shows a low correlation with the US stock market. Their study demonstrates that at the turn of the century the semi-annual All Art Index fell by 8%, while the S&P 500 dropped by 30% due to the global economic downturn. With a low correlation coefficient[3] of 0.04% over the past 50 years, Art serves to act as an effective investment for portfolio diversification. Nonetheless, this can only be achieved if the Art portfolio itself is diversified. Their work is substantiated by Rachel Campbell's more recent study using data from 1965 through to 2002.[4]

Bordeaux wines rose in value by 8.5% in 2002, according to the Decanter Bordeaux Index[5] comprised of some 1,300 wines, compared with a fall of 21% in the FTSE 100 Index over the same period. The Bordeaux Index Ltd has created a credible secondary market. The Bordeaux Index Ltd acts as a market maker agreeing to buy and sell at listed prices, and adjusting prices in line with demand.

The collectibles' market (antiques, art, coins and wine) comprises interesting subjects for economic analysis. This study concentrates on measuring and interpreting the financial return to investing in Fine Wine and its impact on portfolio diversification. In a survey undertaken by Formanek (1991)[6] 22% of respondents gave financial investment as a motivation for their collecting. Collectibles can be a great investment, especially if investors can determine the next growth market.

Producers of cherished collectibles often achieve superior economic profits. Long and Schiffman's (1997)[7] study of the Swatch watch collecting phenomenon, which began in the 1980's and continues today demonstrates how a company can manipulate marketing and production by creating artificial scarcity through limiting production and having different retailers carry different selections. This is an example of turning a commodity into a collectible.

THE RELATIONSHIP BETWEEN PRICE AND QUALITY

Academics advocate that higher quality products should command higher prices. But, when quality cannot be determined in advance of purchase, for example buying wine en primeur, investors must rely on a number of indicators in forming quality expectations. Baum and Powell (1995)[8] and Rao (1994)[9] note that quality ratings made by experts and critics operate as useful indicators in a number of markets. The price of a product is positively correlated to its quality rating if expert opinions are deemed reliable.

One of the greatest influences on the Fine Wine investment market since the great 1982 vintage is the American wine critic Robert Parker, whose most obvious contribution to the literature on wine has been the concept of scoring wine. Parker established his reputation in 1983 by rightly recommending in his newsletter *The Wine Advocate* that readers invest in the 1982 vintage, which has offered investors some of the best returns. Parker has provided a means of scoring wine as a commodity and these scores have become internationally recognised benchmarks. These scores have had a demonstrable effect on individual wine prices, market demand and release price; some believe a wine rated above 90 cannot be bought and wine rated below 80 cannot be sold.

Research into price-quality relationships look beyond the quality rating of the product to consider the producer's history of quality. Shapiro's (1983)[10] model of reputation formation noted that previous demonstrations of quality should translate into a reputation for product quality that is reflected in current prices.

Nelson (1970)[11] introduced the distinction between "search" and "experience" goods. "Search" goods can be defined as goods where the consumer acquires product and vendor information drawing their own conclusions prior to purchase. For experience goods, search is ineffective, and in making their assessments investors rely on expert evaluations and a producer's reputation for quality. Wine is a classic example of an experience good. Thus high quality wines that have a slower maturity rate and whose producers have reputations for quality, command higher prices. Nonetheless, established producers often charge whatever the market will bear. A recent study by The Henley Centre notes that wine was amongst the few commodities where consumers still considered high price to be synonymous with high quality, even in times of economic recession.[12]

THE CASE AGAINST ALTERNATIVE INVESTMENT: STUDIES THAT SUPPORT THE CLAIM THAT ALTERNATIVE INVESTMENTS COMPARE *UNFAVORABLY* WITH TRADITIONAL FINANCIAL INVESTMENTS

A number of academic studies demonstrate that most alternative investments yield lower financial asset returns. Studies that measure volatility over time find that collectibles carry more risk than most financial assets, contending that the risk-adjusted rate of return on alternative investments compares poorly to investments in traditional financial assets.

These studies note that the narrower the alternative investment market being considered, the higher the volatility in financial returns. Pompe (1996)[13] demonstrates that photographs have a return of 30% p.a. after including buyer's fees, but are extremely volatile, with a standard deviation of 300% in annual returns. Baumol (1986)[14] uses the repeat-sales regression method with 640 repeat sales to estimate the real rate of return on paintings over the period from 1652 to 1961 to be only 0.55% p.a.

Frey and Pommerehne (1989)[15] subsequently extend Baumol's data from 1635 to 1987 with 2,396 repeat sales, including sales from more countries, and conclude that paintings are relatively unattractive investments, yielding only 1.4% p.a. between 1635 and 1949 and 1.6% p.a. between 1950 and 1987. They conclude that the real return to art is low relative to the real returns provided by long-term bonds.

Goetzmann (1993)[16] also uses the repeat-sales regression method to the same effect, estimating the returns to paintings, using data from the period 1715 to 1986, are lower than the return to long-term bonds.

Still, from 1850 to 1986, paintings have a higher return and a much higher standard deviation than stocks or long-term bonds. The high returns to art estimated by Goetzmann reflect the fact that this sample period ends in 1986, prior to a collapse in art prices.

Pesando (1993)[17] uses 27,961 repeat sales to construct a price index of modern prints over 1977 to 1992 and finds that the average real rate of return on an aggregate print portfolio was only 1.51% p.a., well below the real return on stocks. His data shows a much higher volatility in Picasso prints than for prints in general. He concludes that the risks associated with investing in prints are comparable to those of stocks or long-term bonds.

Moreover, some studies suggest that alternative investment markets are positively correlated with financial assets markets. Goetzmann (1993) and Chanel (1995)[18] suggest that changes in stock market valuations drive changes in the art market, through the simple mechanism that stock investors become wealthier and spend their gains in part on art or other alternative investments.

Ginsburgh and Jeanfils (1995)[19] find no long-term relationship between art and stocks, but find that in the short-term, financial markets may influence art markets. But despite their findings, the performance of the art market in recent years is unsupportive of the positive correlation argument. Bartholomew (1991)[20] concludes that the early 1990s art market crash was uncorrelated with stock movements and the 1987 stock market crash did not bring about the art market crash.

THE CASE SUPPORTING ALTERNATIVE INVESTMENT: STUDIES THAT SUPPORT THE CLAIM THAT ALTERNATIVE INVESTMENTS COMPARE *FAVORABLY* WITH TRADITIONAL FINANCIAL INVESTMENTS

Academic studies that determine whether returns on various alternative investments are correlated with each other, and with financial asset returns, note that if a negative correlation exists between alternative investments and the stock market, then investors may use collectibles as hedge investments[21]. Ibbotson and Brinson (1987)[22] correlate various alternative investment indices against various financial assets from 1970 to 1985 and find a negative correlation with financial asset returns and conclude that alternative investments can provide a hedge against various financial assets. Cardell et al (1995)[23] conclude that stamps are negatively correlated with stocks over the period from 1947 to 1988, and may serve a potential hedge against stock market risk. Kane (1984)[24] finds that coin returns could have provided a potential hedge during the 1970's and early 1980's. Empirical evidence suggests that the return on collectibles may be negatively correlated with financial asset returns, thereby serving as hedge investments against stock market rises and falls, as the returns on most collectibles remain relatively constant in bear markets.

In his book, *Sold: The Rise and Fall of the House of Sotheby*, Nicholas Faith (1985)[25] writes that the British Rail pension fund was the only real institutional attempt to invest in alternative investments. In 1974, Sotheby's auction house encouraged British Rail to invest in art and by 1979 it held 3% of its total pension fund assets as artworks (Old Master paintings and other classics representing 20% of the value, Brown (1994)[26]). By 1994, the return on the portfolio was 13.8% p.a. during a period when UK stocks averaged 21.5%. In 2003 British Rail sold its last work, in part because prices for art had become seriously high.[27]

Most alternative investment markets exhibit boom-bust patterns in the short-term. Cardell et al. (1995)[28] find a significant price rise and subsequent price fall in stamps during the period from 1978 to 1982. Cutler et al. (1991)[29] see positive correlations in annual returns to collectibles over short horizons and negative correlations over long horizons. These short-term price movements raise the question as to whether insiders in a given alternative investment market make superior returns and then move out before investors move in.

Coffman (1991)[30] defines a "bargain" as buying an undervalued asset and suggests that "bargains" may be found in various tangible assets, most notably art, antiques and wine. He states that unorganized markets, such as for those items sold primarily at auction and yard sales, offer the greatest potential for bargains. But as markets become more organized, the possibility of such bargains declines. Goetzmann (1995)[31] finds that "informational efficiency" has contributed to a decrease in price risk in the art market, and, with Spiegel (1995),[32] suggest that the increasing popularity of alternative investments has led to a reduction in low return realization. According to Ashenfelter (1989),[33] prices converge over time between wine markets in New York, London and Amsterdam, and have apparent arbitrage opportunities between New York and Geneva (although un-exploitable due to trade barriers). Ginsburgh and Jeanfils (1995)[34] observe that although various auction markets in New York, London and Paris move together, there does not appear to be significant arbitrage opportunities across international auction markets.

THE PERFORMANCE AND INVESTMENT POTENTIAL OF FINE WINE

The empirical evidence presented in the previous section suggests that alternative investments do not yield greater returns than traditional financial assets, especially when the volatility of returns and transaction costs are taken into account. Academic studies that calculate the rate of return on alternative asset classes conclude, with few exceptions, that non-financial assets are not good investments. But in the case of Fine Wine, the evidence is inconclusive; some have claimed that the rate of return on Fine Wine investment is comparable to or exceeds the return on equities and bonds. Even so, economists and academics have still not reached a consensus on the relative attractiveness of wine as a serious alternative investment.

Krasker (1979)[35] concludes that wine is a bad investment because the estimated 5.9% p.a. return between 1973 and 1977 was less than the US Treasury bill rate at the time; and net of storage costs, this return falls to negative 8% p.a. Weil (1993)[36] analyzes transactions in an investor's wine portfolio from 1978 to 1992 and calculates a nominal rate of return of 8% p.a., well below the nominal New York Stock Exchange return averaging 15% p.a.

But Thomas (1998)[37] claims that wine outperformed the FTSE 100 Index and the Dow Jones Index throughout the 1990s, and Graeser (1993)[38] suggests that although alternative investments are generally poor long-term investments, Fine Wine constitutes an exception and has the potential to yield superior returns over similarly risky financial assets. In the 1980s and 1990s some blue chip wines yielded above average returns suggesting that wine ought to be considered a serious alternative investment. Jaeger, by modifying Krasker's (1979)[39] storage cost estimate downwards and using a longer time period that bridges recessions, demonstrates that from 1969 to 1977 wine yields a substantial premium over the risk free rate. He concludes that the financial performance of wine outperformed US Treasury bills by 16.6%. Bryon and Ashenfelter (1995)[40] find that Fine Wine in their sample yielded a reasonable rate of return of between 3.3% and 4.6% over the period from 1966 to 1991.

Burton and Jacobsen (2001)[41] use a more recent time period from 1986 to 1996 that spans both recessionary and expansionary periods, and employ the repeat-sales regression method, with 10,558 repeat sales that allow for "within-period" and "full-period" return calculations. They find that the average nominal rate of return for this period was 7.9% p.a. and the corresponding real rate of return was 3.1% p.a. During the same period the Dow Jones Industrial Average (DJIA) increased an average of 13.5% p.a., not including dividends that were paid out, and the one-year Treasury bill yielded a nominal rate of 5.8% p.a. The wine portfolio outperforms the Treasury bill portfolio but underperforms against the equities portfolio. Burton and Jacobsen note that between 1986 and 1996 the volatility of returns to wine compare unfavorably with the volatility of traditional financial assets; and considerable negative returns are followed by significant positive returns. The standard deviation of the semi-annual returns for wine of 0.13 exceeded that for the DJIA and one-year T-bills of 0.08 and 0.01 respectively. Since 1993, investment in wine yielded a nominal return of 15.5% p.a. well below the nominal equity return of 19.3% p.a. over the same period.

Some writers contend that the rate of return to wine is specific to the time period under scrutiny, and that the return is deemed artificial if there is a depression in the wine market, as evidenced in the 1980's; Jaeger (1981)[42] notes that wine is fairly demand-elastic and the return on wine is relatively sensitive to the period that is being studied. Wine critic Steven Spurrier (1997)[43] describes the current state of the market as "auction fever," stressing that the wine market is best characterised as a speculative bubble.

Other wine critics are more positive than Spurrier. Hugh Johnson (1971)[44] suggests buying wine young at its opening price and holding onto it until it reaches maturity in order to achieve superior returns. Frank Prial (1997)[45] of *The New York Times* and Alexandra Peers (1997)[46] of *The Wall Street Journal* both comment on the significant price appreciation experienced by specific blue chip wines and specific vintages. Auction correspondent for the leading US wine journal *Wine Spectator*, Peter Meltzer (1997),[47] notes that the wine market frequently outperforms the Dow Jones Industrial Average and recent articles in *The Wall Street Journal* and *The Financial Times* encourage investors to include wine in their investment portfolios. *Zachys Gazette*,[48] a leading wine retailer's advertising feature published in *The New York Times*, reports that top Bordeaux prices increased in the auction market by 25 to 50% p.a. from 1987 to 1997.

However, there have been instances where wine has sold for less than the highest price received when sold late in its lifecycle, a declining price anomaly.[49] Grimond (1998)[50] notes that investors should anticipate which wines are going to be in high demand in the future and then invest heavily in those wines as opposed to simply holding a well-diversified portfolio. Wine investors may become more informed over time about the quality of successive vintages, which tends to drive up the initial price of good vintages.

Sokolin (1987)[51] specifically considers wine's investment potential by creating 3 classes of investment grade wine and suggests investors should hold a variety of wines from different producers and vintages for maximum diversification. Grade 1 wines offer the best combination of risk and return, yielding a nominal return of 7.7% p.a. compared to grades 2 and 3, yielding 7.2% and 5.3% respectively. His 1985 portfolio, bought in early 1986 at a futures price, provides the opportunity to simulate returns based on actual figures at the beginning of the sample period. The "average" auction prices yielded 9.4% p.a. and "maximum" auction prices 11.8% p.a., providing better returns than investing only in first growth wines. Parker (1985)[52] specifically considers 15 Châteaux worthy of first growth designation. The nominal growth for all vintages for these Châteaux is 7.8% p.a., but higher returns are achieved for those investing in only 1961 or 1982 vintages from these Châteaux yielding nominal returns of 9.9% p.a. and 16.2% p.a. respectively.

In a well-functioning capital market, risk adjusted rates of return on different assets should equal one another through arbitrage.[53] The equilibrium rate of return on fine wine, net of incidental costs, should equal the net equilibrium return on competing assets with identical risk. But given the costs associated with trading and holding wine, it is unclear whether the rate of return on wine should be less than the return on similarly risky assets in financial markets.

THE EFFECT ON THE RATE OF RETURN OF INCIDENTAL COSTS AND BENEFITS

Some academics have detected a substantial differential between gross and net returns on alternative investments, given the need to use market makers like auction houses and dealers to buy and sell collectibles. Studies that take into account these costs and other incidental transportation and holding costs find that the rate of return may fall. Burton and Jacobsen (2001)[54] calculate for a specific wine portfolio that sales commissions and insurance costs reduce a gross return rate in the range of 9.4% to 11.8% by 3.7%.

On the other hand, the tax advantages can offset these costs and constitute potentially significant benefits to the investor (Frey (1997))[55]. In the UK, wine is a tax-exempt asset with a life expectancy of less than 50 years, and investors are exempt from Capital Gains Tax. In the United States, the usual Capital Gains Tax may apply as with other collectibles. Traders who frequently buy or sell wine are tax-liable, but the situation is less clear if a private individual sells wine at auction. Another option is to donate the wine at its appraised value and take a tax write off by setting it against tax liabilities—an attractive option to high-income owners and popular in the US—but since other assets can also be donated, this may not necessarily improve the rate of return on wine relative to other assets.

Transaction costs on both buying and selling wine at auction can also be substantial. For example, commissions are charged for both buying (10-15%) and selling (15%) although the seller's commission varies according to the total value of the consignment. It may be possible to reduce these costs by selling wine through a dealer, private sale, or by going directly to the buyer. Sokolin (1987)[56] downplays these ideas as viable options, contending that most retailers are reluctant to buy from private investors.

Sellers occasionally incur catalogue related charges at auctions for a write up on their consignment. Another transaction cost that would deter the small-consignment seller is that they must frequently offer several tasting bottles. On the buyer's side, the premium charged on top of all auction prices is a significant expense that, to lessen its effects on returns, requires long-term holding of wine to amortise it sufficiently. Smaller, less established auction houses sometimes waive either the buyer or seller premiums to attract business. Moreover, holding wine, whether at a private dwelling or at a distributor's premises, incurs shipping, storage and insurance costs, expenditures that are far more difficult to quantify.

Sokolin (1987) goes on to demonstrate that a portfolio consisting of only 1982 vintage would beat the DJIA or the FTSE 100 with an actual net return of 16.2% after taking these sales commissions and associated costs into account. Nonetheless, the relative attractiveness of Sokolin's futures portfolio diminishes after a 15% sales commission, 1% insurance charge, and storage costs of $1.50 per month per case for a 120-month holding period (assuming the wine was immediate delivery after the future is purchased) reduces the net nominal return substantially from 9.4% p.a. to 5.7% p.a. under the "average" auction price scenario and from 11.8% p.a. to 8.4% p.a. under the "maximum" auction price scenario.

Other academics contend that there are some alternative investments achieving high and some achieving low rates of return, although, as already mentioned, the evidence is not conclusive as to whether Fine Wine constitutes a viable alternative investment to traditional financial assets.[57] There is evidence to suggest that Fine Wine could be considered a serious alternative investment that compares favorably to an investment in equities and fixed income securities.

ENDNOTES

1. Bawden, A., "Alternative Investments: Tangible Assets With Less of a String Attached," *Financial Times*, May 25, 2002 .

2. Mei, J., & Moses, M., *Art Investment*, Stern School of Business, New York University, 2001.

3. The riskiness of a portfolio of 2 assets depends on the sign and size of the correlation coefficient. If the correlation coefficient is +1, the returns for the 2 assets are perfectly positively related and the asset returns always move in the same direction, but not necessarily by the same percentage amount. In this case the risk cannot be reduced through diversification. If the correlation is –1, the converse applies and portfolio risk can be eliminated through diversification. If the correlation coefficient is zero, the asset returns are not related and risk can be reduced through diversification but it will not be eliminated.

4. Campbell, R., *The Art of Portfolio Diversification*, Maastricht University, 2004.

5. Robinson, J., & Boom, G., "2003 Head to Head," *Decanter*, January, 2003.

6. Formanek, R., "Why They Collect: Collectors Reveal Their Motivations," *Journal of Social Behaviour & Personality* 6:6, 1991, pp. 275–286.

7. Long, M.M., & Schiffman, L.G., "Swatch Fever: An Allegory for Understanding the Paradox of Collecting," *Psychology & Marketing* 14:5, , 1997, pp. 495–509.

8. Baum, J.A.C., & Powell, W.W., "Cultivating an Institutional Ecology of Organisation," *American Journal of Sociology* 60, 1995 , pp. 529–538.

9. Rao, H., "The Social Construction of Reputation: 1895–1912," *Strategic Management Journal* 15, 1994, pp. 29–44.

10. Shapiro, C., "Premiums for High Quality Products as Returns to Reputations," *Quarterly Journal of Economics* 98, 1983, pp. 659–679.

11. Nelson, P., "Information and Consumer Behaviour," *Journal of Political Economy* 78, 1970, 19 pages.

12. The Henley Centre, Consumer Research Unit, 1993.

13. Pompe, J., "An Investment Flash: The Rate of Return for Photographs," *Southern Economic Journal* 63:2, 1996, pp. 488–495.

14. Baumol, W., "Unnatural Value: Or Art Investment as Floating Crap Game," *American Economic Review* 76, 1986, pp. 10–14.

15. Frey, B., & Pommerehne, W., "Art Investment: An Empirical Inquiry," *Southern Economic Journal* 56, 1989, pp. 396–409.

16 . Goetzmann, W.N., "Accounting for Taste: Art and the Financial Markets over Three Centuries," *American Economic Review* 83, 1993, pp. 1370–76.

17. Pesando, J.E., "Art as an Investment: The Market for Modern Prints," *American Economic Review* 83 (5), 1993, page 1075–1089, 15 pp.

18. Chanel, O., "Is Art Market Behaviour Predictable?" *European Economic Review* 39, 1995, pp. 519–27.

19. Ginsburgh, V., & Jeanfils, P., "Long–Term Comovements in International Markets for Paintings," *European Economic Review* 39:3-4, 1995, pp. 538–548.

20. Bartholomew, J., "Collectibles: State of the Art," *Far Eastern Economic Review* 154, 1991, pp. 37–38

21. Hedge investments reduce or eliminate the exposure to risk.
22. Ibbotson, R.G., & Brinson, G.P., *Investment Markets: Gaining the Performance Advantage*, McGraw-Hill, New York, 1st Edition, 1987.
23. Cardell, N.S., Kling, J.L., & Petry, G., "Stamp Returns and Economic Factors," *Southern Economic Journal* 62:2, 1995, pp. 411–427.
24. Kane, A., "Coins: Anatomy of a Fad Asset," *Journal of Portfolio Management* 1:2, 1984, pp. 44–51.
25. Faith, N., *Sold: The Rise and Fall of the House of Sotheby*, Macmillan Publishing Company, New York, 1st Edition, 1985, pp. 208–218.
26. Brown, C., "Art for Money's Sake," *Forbes*, December 5, 1994.
27. "Art for Money's Sake," *The Economist*, May 27, 2004, 1 page.
28. Cardell, N.S., Kling, J.L., & Petry, G., "Stamp Returns and Economic Factors," *Southern Economic Journal* 62:2, 1995, pp. 411–427.
29. Cutler, D.M., Poterba, J.M., & Summers, L.M., "Speculative Dynamics," *Review of Economic Studies* 58:3, 1991, pp. 529–546.
30. Coffman, R.B., "Art Investment and Asymmetrical Information," *Journal of Cultural Economics* 15:2, 1991, pp. 83–94.
31. Goetzmann, W.N., "The Informational Efficiency of the Art Market," *Managerial Finance* 21:6, 1995, pp. 25–34.
32. Goetzmann, W.N., & Spiegel, M., "Private Value Components, and the Winner's Curse in an Art Index," *European Economic Review* 39, 1995, pp. 549–555.
33. Ashenfelter, O., "How Auctions Work for Wine & Art," *Journal of Economic Perspectives* 3, 1989 , pp. 23–36.
34. Ginsburgh, V., & Jeanfils, P., "Long-Term Comovements in International Markets for Paintings," *European Economic Review* 39:3–4, 1995, pp. 538–548.
35. Krasker, W., "The Rate of Return to Storing Wines", *Journal of Political Economy* 87, 1979, 5 pp..
36. Weil, R.L., "Do Not Invest in Wine, At Least in the US, Unless You Plan to Drink It, and Maybe Not Even Then, or As An Investment, Wine is No Corker," *Paper Presented at the 2nd International Conference of the Vineyard Quantification Society*, 1993, Verona, Italy.
37. Thomas, M., "Alternative Investing: Wine Collectors Drive Up Prices," *Business News New Jersey (North)*, January 19, 1998.
38. Graeser, P., "Rate of Return to Investment in American Antique Furniture," *Southern Economic Journal* 59, 1993, pp. 817–821.
39. Krasker, W., "The Rate of Return to Storing Wines," *Journal of Political Economy* 87, 1979, pp. 1363–1367.
40. Byron, R.P., & Ashenfelter, O., "Predicting the Quality of an Unborn Grange," *Economic Record* 71, 1995, pp. 40–53.
41. Burton, B.J., & Jacobsen, J.P., "The Rate of Return on Investment in Wine," *Economic Inquiry* 39, 2001, pp. 337–350.
42. Jaeger, E., "To Save or Savour: The Rate of Return to Storing Wine," *Journal of Political Economy* 89, 1981, pp. 584–592.
43. Spurrier, S., "Auction Fever: Can Prices Rise Forever?" *Decanter*, December, 1997.
44. Johnson, H. *The World Atlas of Wine*, Simon & Schuster, New York, 1st Edition, 1971.

45. Prial, F.J., "Bordeaux Again Leads a High-Price Parade," *New York Times*, September 17, 1997.

46. Peers, A., "Hot Cellars: Wine Prices are Soaring," *Wall Street Journal*, May 2, 1997.

47. Meltzer, P., "Third Quarter Gains Nearly Double Previous Results," *Wine Spectator*, Dec. 31, 1997, 2 pages.

48. New York Times, September 9, 1997.

49. Ashenfelter, O., "How Auctions Work for Wine & Art," *Journal of Economic Perspectives*, 1989, 14 pages.

50. Grimond, M., "A Vintage Year to Bottle Up Fine Profits in Your Cellar," *Business Day*, January 12, 1998.

51. Sokolin, W., *Liquid Assets*, Macmillan, New York, 1st Edition, 1987.

52. Parker, R., *Bordeaux: The Definitive Guide for the Wines Produced since 1961*, Simon & Schuster, New York, 1st Edition, 1985.

53. Bodie, Z., & Kane, A., & Marcus, A.J., *Investments*, McGraw-Hill/Irwin, New York, 5th Edition, 2002.

54. Burton, B.J., & Jacobsen, J.P., "The Rate of Return on Investment in Wine," *Economic Inquiry* 39, 2001, pp. 337–350.

55. Frey, B.S., "Art Markets & Economics: Introduction," *Journal of Cultural Economics*, 1997, 9 pages.

56. Sokolin, W., *Liquid Assets*, Macmillan, New York, 1st Edition, 1987.

57. Burton, B.J., & Jacobsen, J.P., "Measuring Returns on Investment in Collectables," *Journal of Economic Perspectives* 13, 1999, pp. 193–212.

3

CRITICAL REVIEW OF PORTFOLIO THEORY AND DIVERSIFICATION

CRITICAL REVIEW OF MODERN PORTFOLIO THEORY

In the traditional Markowitz (1952)[1] model, investors maximize returns subject to a volatility constraint. Portfolios are chosen on the basis of the expected returns (ER_p) and variance in returns (V_p), and each investor maximizes an objective function, $U = ER_p - ZV_p$, where U represents the utility value assigned to the portfolio and Z is a positive constant, which measures risk aversion.[2] The objective is therefore to maximize expected return and minimize risk in order to maximise investors' utility. This is the mean-variance optimization goal underlying the Markowitz theory and represents a trade-off between desired return and acceptable risk. The assumption is that investors prefer more return and less risk, and select portfolios that offer a higher return for the same risk or a lower risk for the same return. Optimal investment for a single period entails finding the minimum-risk portfolio for all possible expected returns, using data on variances and covariances and expectations of asset returns and then selecting one that maximizes the objective function, or one best suited to the investors' preference.[3] The optimum portfolio follows from the combination of the objective function and the minimum-risk constraint. Modern Portfolio Theory works out the best combination of assets to hold in a portfolio of risky assets and assumes investors are trying to combine assets to get the best return relative to the riskiness of the overall portfolio. The process of selecting the optimal portfolio involves the separation property theorem that consists of two independent tasks:[4] first, the technical aspects in determining the optimal portfolio, and second, the asset allocation decision between risk free and risky investment. The mean-variance model clearly shows that there is an optimal portfolio that operates on the presence of a volatility constraint.

The risk-return profile of all assets and portfolios is shown in Figure 3.1[5]. This is the feasible set representing all portfolios, which can be formed from a group of "n" assets in which an efficient[6] set of portfolios can be derived. The first stage of the optimal portfolio selection process requires segmenting those portfolios with the highest return for the same risk, or the lowest risk for the same return from the feasible set.

FIGURE 3.1

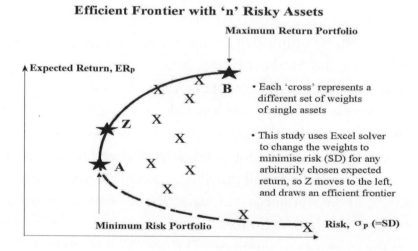

Efficient Frontier with 'n' Risky Assets

Figure 3.1 shows the minimum-risk portfolio, furthest in direction to decreasing risk and the maximum-return portfolio, highest in direction to increasing returns. In both cases there is no portfolio that has less risk for the same return, or more return for the same risk, satisfying the mean-variance criteria. The efficient frontier is the curve containing the set of efficient portfolios between point A and B. It exhibits the classic risk-return relationship where higher return expectations are associated with higher risk.

The expected return (ER_p) for a two-asset class portfolio can be written arithmetically as:

$ER_p = (W_1 * ER_1) + (W_2 * ER_2)$, where ER_p is the portfolio expected return, ER_1 and ER_2 the expected return of asset 1 and asset 2 respectively and proportions $W_1 + W_2 = 1$.

The risk of a single asset is the variance or standard deviation (s). The risk of a portfolio of assets depends on the covariance and correlation between the returns. The level of diversification depends on how low the correlation is between the assets. The less they co-vary the more risk is reduced. This is shown in Figure 3.2.

FIGURE 3.2

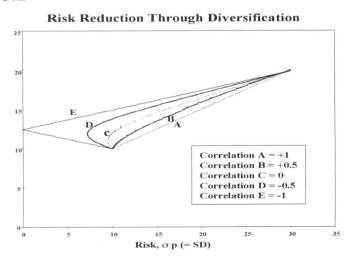

Risk Reduction Through Diversification

Correlation A = +1
Correlation B = +0.5
Correlation C = 0
Correlation D = -0.5
Correlation E = -1

Risk, σp (= SD)

The variance of a two-asset class portfolio (s^2_p) can be written arithmetically as:

$s^2_p = W_1^2 * s^2_1 + W_2^2 * s^2_2 + (2 * W_1 * W_2 * s_{12})$, where s^2_p is the portfolio variance and $s_{12} = r_{12} * s_1 * s_2$

Thus $s^2_p = W_1^2 * s^2_1 + W_2^2 * s^2_2 + (2 * W_1 * W_2 * r_{12} * s_1 * s_2)$, where s_1 and s_2 are the standard deviations of asset 1 and asset 2 respectively and r_{12} is the covariance between asset 1 and asset 2. The standard deviation of the portfolio is the square root of the portfolio variance.

The weight of any risky asset decreases as risk aversion increases. The efficient frontier of risky assets can be found by solving a non-linear optimization problem. Depending on how much risk an investor is willing to take, a portfolio should be chosen on the efficient frontier with an acceptable level of risk. The main limitation to identifying the optimal portfolio is that investors need to know the correlations between all risky assets, and for each investor or for each level of risk there is a new optimization problem to be solved. Nobel Prize winner James Tobin resolved this limitation in 1958 by demonstrating that investors could invest in portfolios that combined a risk free asset with a portfolio of risky assets.

At this point, stage two of the optimal portfolio selection process must take place in order to obtain a single optimal portfolio. The model is developed on the assumption that all investors are able to borrow and lend at the same risk free interest rate. Thus, if 'W' were the proportion of wealth invested in the risky asset portfolio, then '1-W' would be the proportion invested in the risk free rate. The expected return for the investment in a risky portfolio and the risk free asset can be written arithmetically as:

$ER_p = (W * ER_{rp}) + ((1-W) * ER_{rf})$, where ER_{rp} is the expected return on the risky portfolio and ER_{rf} is the expected return on the risk free asset.

The variance for the investment in a risky portfolio and the risk free asset can be written arithmetically as:

$s^2_p = (W^2 * s^2_{rp}) + ((1-W)^2 * s^2_{rf}) + (2 * W * (1-W) * s_{rp} * s_{rf} * r_{rprf})$, where s_{rp} and s_{rf} are the standard deviations of the risky assets and the risk free asset respectively and r_{rprf} is the covariance between the risky portfolio and the risk free asset.

On the basis that the risk free asset has a standard deviation of zero, the following equation is derived:

$s^2_p = [W^2 * s^2_{rp}]$ taking the square root $s_p = [W^2 * s^2_{rp}]^- = W * s_{rp}$ thus, $W = s_p / s_{rp}$

By substituting W into the equation for ER_p (where $ER_p = (W * ER_{rp}) + (1-W) * EF_{rf})$) the following equation is derived:

$ER_p = (s_p / s_{rp}) * ER_{rp} + [1 - (s_p / s_{rp})] * ER_{rf}$ where $ER_p = (s_p / s_{rp}) * (ER_{rp} - ER_{rf}) + ER_{rf}$

The gradient of the straight line is the Sharpe ratio of the portfolio (excess return per unit of risk) whilst the intercept of the line is the risk free rate of return. Investors are allowed to borrow or lend at the risk free rate and invest in any single risky portfolio on the efficient frontier. For each single risky portfolio, this gives a new set of risk-return combinations. Figure 3 shows the Transformation Line: a straight line that is simply the combination of any single risky portfo-lio and the safe asset. Each risky asset portfolio has its own transfor-mation line, and investors can move along this transformation line by altering one's borrowing or lending.

FIGURE 3.3

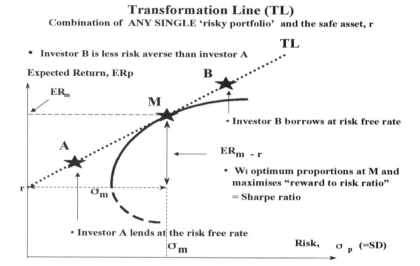

Transformation Line (TL)
Combination of ANY SINGLE 'risky portfolio' and the safe asset, r

At this stage, in order to find the portfolio weights—the most optimal combination of risky assets and a risk free asset—the transformation line must be rotated in a counter-clockwise position as far as possible. This would be the point where the line is tangent to the efficient frontier. The line derived is the Capital Market Line (CML), the highest achievable transformation line.

The aggregate supply of all risky assets in the market is the market portfolio (M). In equilibrium (i.e. where there is an optimal risk and return combination) investors want a transformation line equal to the market portfolio. The optimal weighted portfolio maximises the Sharpe ratio. Non-optimal portfolios i.e. badly weighted portfolios lie below the CML. It follows that all investors will select the same portfolio of risky assets, the market portfolio (M). At the time investors choose optimal proportions, investors can expect to obtain a reward to risk ratio of, $S = (ER_m - r) / s_m$ (see figure 3.4).

FIGURE 3.4

Capital Market Line (CML)

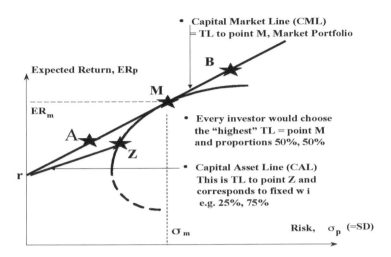

Figure 3.4 shows that further down the CML investors would lend at the risk free rate and invest part wealth in risky assets and further up the CML investors would borrow at the risk free rate and invest all wealth in risky assets. The proportions held in either are the same but the monetary amounts are not the same.

CRITICAL REVIEW OF PORTFOLIO DIVERSIFICATION

William Sharpe (1963/64)[7], John Lintner (1965)[8] and Jan Mossin (1966)[9] demonstrated that the market portfolio is an efficient portfolio that lies on the efficient frontier. In equilibrium, the only portfolio of risky assets that investors hold is the market portfolio, and since all investors hold the market portfolio, the risk of an individual asset is characterized by its correlation with respect to the market. The beta (b) of an asset is a measure of its co-movement with the market portfolio, relative to the total volatility of the return on the market portfolio. When balanced, investing in a riskless asset and the market portfolio is an efficient portfolio strategy.

The total risk of a portfolio is measured by the variance or standard deviation of portfolio returns. The variance of portfolio returns is denoted by s^2_p, and can be written arithmetically as:

$$s^2_p = (b^2_{pi} * s^2_i) + s^2e_p$$

The right-hand side of the equation denoted by "$b^2_{pi} * s^2_i$" reflects the sum of the systematic or market risk and the idiosyncratic or unique risk denoted by "s^2e_p". Market forces drive systematic risk and examples include interest rate risk, purchasing power risk, exchange rate risk and political risk. Idiosyncratic risk is unique to a specific firm or industry, examples of which are business risk, financial risk, default risk and liquidity risk.

Beta (b) is a measure of systematic risk. Increasing the number of assets in a portfolio does not reduce the portfolio beta or systematic risk, but reduces idiosyncratic risk, defined as the volatility of an asset's return that is uncorrelated with the total portfolio. The more diversified the portfolio, the lower the idiosyncratic risk. For a well-diversified portfolio, the volatility of each asset contributes little to portfolio risk. In the case where the random error component of assets are assumed to be uncorrelated and where the investments in all assets are equal, the proportion W_i, representing the weights of each asset class$_i$ will equal 1/n, where n is the number of assets (see figure 3.5).

FIGURE 3.5

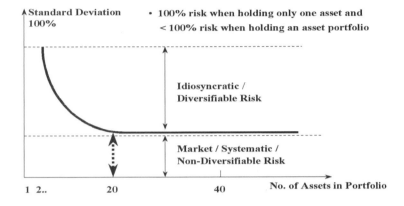

Random Selection of Assets

Increasing the size (= n) of the portfolio

(each asset has 'weight' wᵢ = 1/n)

Modern Portfolio Theory holds that diversification of assets within the domestic market eliminates idiosyncratic risk but not systematic risk. International diversification results from the relatively low correlations between asset returns in international markets, and consequently improves the risk-return characteristics of a portfolio. The theory advocates that the inclusion of international assets shifts the efficient frontier of the optimal portfolio upwards, enhancing the Sharpe ratio.[10]

Countries differ significantly in their cultural, political, economic and financial characteristics and the greater the differences between economies, the lower the correlations in international financial markets. Most markets have correlations in the range of 0.4 to 0.7,[11] and since these correlations are less than 1, diversification benefits may be achieved. The impact of global diversification is greatest where there is a longer investment horizon, as correlations tend to be lower over longer holding periods.[12] Diversifying away idiosyncratic risk eliminates 70% of the total portfolio risk.[13] Holding a well-diversified portfolio of assets reduces idiosyncratic risk to zero. This supports the much-tested hypothesis that approximately 20 to 30 assets constitute a well-diversified portfolio. Systematic risk accounts for 30% of the total portfolio risk and cannot be diversified since each individual asset in the portfolio is affected to some extent by market fluctuations (see figure 3.6).

FIGURE 3.6

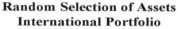

**Random Selection of Assets
International Portfolio**

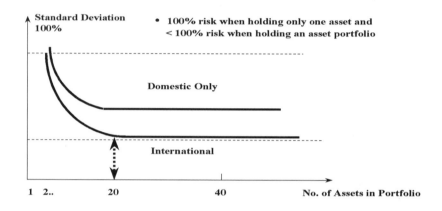

CRITICAL REVIEW OF LITERATURE ON PORTFOLIO DIVERSIFICATION

Virtually all asset-pricing models claim that a diversified investor does not expect compensation for holding idiosyncratic risk. Diversified investors are uncompensated for idiosyncratic risk since the idiosyncratic risk is diversified away as the number of assets in a portfolio increases. Therefore most rational models of investor choice suggest that investors hold diversified portfolios to reduce systematic risk. In a recent study on asset portfolio diversification Goetzmann and Kumar (2001)[14] examined the performance of more than 40,000 portfolios from 1991 to 1996, and conclude that most investors tend to under-diversify. Investors realize the benefits of diversification but adopt a "naïve" diversification strategy and construct portfolios with little regard to the correlations between the assets. The average number of assets in investor portfolios increased and the correlation between assets in the US market fell, thereby enhancing portfolio diversification and reducing portfolio variance. Some advocate that c.20 to 30 assets are sufficient to get near-maximum diversification benefits. But the observed level of diversification in this study is much lower; 25% of portfolios contained only 1 asset; 50% contained 3 or fewer assets; and only 5-10% contained more than 10 assets.

According to Rode (2000),[15] investors realise the benefits of diversification, but find it difficult to implement and maintain a well-diversified portfolio. Investors often use simple "rules of thumb" to form their portfolios. Biarritz and Thayer (2001)[16] suggest that investors most often use simple diversification techniques, notably the 1/n rule, when formulating their asset allocation decisions. The 1/n rule states that simple diversification occurs by holding many assets where n is the number of assets where the sum of the weighting of each of the assets is equal to 1 or 100%. Holding many independent uncorrelated assets of similar size diversifies risk tending towards zero. Markowitz diversification uses an analytical portfolio diversification technique to maximize portfolio returns for a particular level of risk, which is less intuitive than simple diversification. In constructing portfolios investors commonly use intuition, simple correlations, simple portfolio theory, and the Capital Asset Pricing Model.[17] It is possible that investors under-diversify due to the small size of their portfolio. Investors holding big portfolios are likely to be better diversified because they hold a greater number of assets and consequently achieve higher risk adjusted returns.

Theories explaining investor under-diversification are not in short supply. Merton (1987)[18] suggests that search and monitoring costs often force investors to reduce the number of assets in their portfolios and Depend (1998)[19] proposes the notion that investors believe they can manage portfolio risk better by understanding a small number of assets. Kroll, Levy, and Rapport (1988)[20] find that investors tend to ignore correlations between assets when constructing portfolios. Huberman (2001)[21] finds that investors have a strong tendency to invest in assets that they are most familiar with. Odeon (1999)[22] finds that over-confident investors often wrongly believe they can achieve superior returns by active trading and consequently choose not to diversify. Kelly (1995)[23] suggests that over-confidence can emerge among investors simply because they may believe that their asset-picking abilities are superior to that of the market.

The sole function of Modern Portfolio Theory is to find a portfolio that is optimal over a single investment period. How should investors choose an initial portfolio that is optimal not just over one period but over the investor's entire investment horizon? How can investors determine a portfolio that is dynamically optimal? Merton (1970s)[24] suggested that over several different investment periods the optimal portfolio has two components: one that is optimal for a single-period investor which lies on the efficient frontier, and one that provides the best hedge against future changes in the efficient frontier. Campbell and Viscera (2002)[25] conclude that static portfolio analysis is not only inappropriate, but can be seriously misleading when investment opportunities are time-varying and investors have long-term horizons.

CRITICAL REVIEW OF OPTIMAL ASSET WEIGHTS AND THE CAPITAL ASSET PRICING MODEL

Asset weights that are negative imply short selling. The portfolio standard deviation where short selling is allowed is smaller. This study negates short selling[26] by forcing the weights in a positive direction. This is shown in Figure 3.7.

FIGURE 3.7

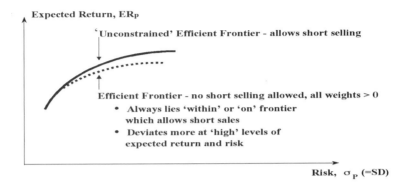

**Efficient Frontier
No Short Selling Allowed**

The optimal weights are sensitive to small changes in the expected return. If estimates of returns are incorrect, the actual risk-return outcome may be very different from that envisaged at the outset. Brittan-Jones (1999)[27] contends that relatively small errors in inputs often produce large errors in portfolios selected. To overcome this sensitivity problem investors may choose weights that minimize portfolio variance. The weights are then independent of expected returns.

Holding a single asset, where its own variance is high (high own variance), is risky and taken on its own investors expect a high return, which compensates the investor for idiosyncratic risk that can be diversified away if the asset is held as part of a portfolio. If the return on this single asset co-varies minutely or negatively with the rest of the assets in the portfolio, then holding this asset may reduce overall portfolio variance. Negative covariances showing low expected returns are acceptable, and positive covariances showing higher expected returns are acceptable. An individual asset's beta is proportional to this covariance, and the CAPM signifies that investors are willing to hold risky assets with high own variances, providing they have small betas, which helps reduce overall portfolio risk.

The CAPM states that only an asset's beta is rewarded, and the return on any asset is the risk-free rate plus the beta multiplied by the market risk premium. Asset pricing is important because it helps investors avoid or sell over-priced assets, exploit or buy under-priced assets, and adjust expected returns to include expected price correlations. The CAPM holds that all correctly priced assets should lie on the SML, which gives the risk-adjusted expected return on an asset or asset portfolio, so that investors are willing to hold the asset or asset portfolio as part of their diversified portfolio. This is shown in Figure 3.8.

FIGURE 3.8

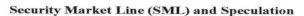

Security Market Line (SML) and Speculation

CAPM implies all 'correctly priced' assets should lie on the SML

SML = Bigger the beta the bigger the expected return

Beta of market portfolio must =1

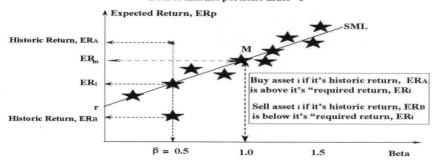

If the asset's historic expected return is equal to the expected return given by the CAPM, then the asset's return accurately reflects its portfolio market risk; investors should hold these assets because they gain returns equal to their contribution to the risk of the overall portfolio. If the historic return is greater than the CAPM return, then investors should buy or invest in these assets, because the asset gives a return greater than its contribution to risk of the overall portfolio. If the historic return is less than the CAPM expected return, then investors should sell or not invest in those assets, because the asset gives a return less than its contribution to risk of the overall portfolio. If an investor holds an asset with a return that is less than the risk-free rate, so long as the beta or the correlation with the market is zero or negative, this asset will reduce overall portfolio risk.

ENDNOTES

1. Markowitz, H., "Portfolio Selection," *Journal of Finance*, March, 1952.
2. Goldsmith, D., "Transaction Costs and the Theory of Portfolio Selection," *Journal of Finance*, Vol. XXXI, No. 4, 1976, pp. 1127–1140.
3. Lee, S.M., & Lerro, A.J., "Optimising the Portfolio Selection for Mutual Funds," *Journal of Finance*, Vol 28, No.5, 1973, pp. 1087–1102
4. Bodie, Z., Kane, A., & Marcus, A.J., *Investments*, McGraw-Hill/Irwin, New York, 5th Edition, 2002.
5. Figures 1-8 extracted from Cuthbertson, K., & Nitzsche, *Investments: Spot & Derivatives Markets*, John Wiley & Sons Ltd, Sussex, 1st Edition, 2001. The graphs have been amended for the purposes of this study.
6. Efficient means the highest expected return for a given level of risk, or the lowest risk for a given return.
7. Sharpe, W., "A Simplified Model of Portfolio Analysis," *Management Science*, January, 1963, Sharpe, W., "Capital Asset Prices: A Theory of Market Equilibrium," *Journal of Finance*, September, 1964.
8. Linter, J., "The Valuation of Risky Assets and the Selection of Risky Investments in Stock Portfolios and Capital Budgets," *Review of Economics and Statistics*, February, 1965.
9. Mossin, J., "Equilibrium in a Capital Asset Market," *Econometrica*, October, 1966.
10. The Sharpe ratio is the ratio of expected return to volatility or risk as measured by its standard deviation.
11. Davis, E.P., Steil, B., *Institutional Investors*, The MIT Press, Cambridge, Massachusetts, US, 1st Edition, 2001.
12. Ibbotson, R.G., "Global Asset Allocation: Philosophy, Process and Performance," *Journal of Investing* 9 (1), 2000, p. 39.
13. Cuthbertson, K., & Nitzsche, *Investments: Spot & Derivatives Markets*, John Wiley & Sons Ltd, Sussex, 1st Edition, 2001.
14. Goetzmann, W.N., & Kumar, A., "Equity Portfolio Diversification," *National Bureau of Economic Research*, Working Paper Number 8686, 2001, 44 pages.
15. Rode, D., "Portfolio Choice and Perceived Diversification," *Working Paper: Department of Social and Decision Sciences*, Carnegie Mellon University, 2000.
16. Benartzi & Thaler, "How Much is Investor Autonomy Worth," *National Bureau of Economic Research*, 2001, 5 pages.

17. The Capital Asset Pricing Model or CAPM gives a benchmark risk-adjusted expected return.

18. Merton, R. C., "A Simple Model of Capital Market Equilibrium with Incomplete Information", *Journal of Finance* 42, 1987, pp. 483–510.

19. DeBondt, W., "A Portrait of the Individual Investor," *European Economic Review* 42, 1998, 14 pages.

20. Kroll, Y., Levy, H., & Rapoport, A., "Experimental Tests of the Separation of Theorem and the Capital Asset Pricing Model," *American Economic Review* 78, 1988, pp. 500–519.

21. Huberman, G., "Familiarity Breeds Investment," *Review of Financial Studies* 14, 2001, pp. 659–680.

22. Odean, T., "Do Investors Trade Too Much?" *American Economic Review* 89, 1999, pp. 1279–1298.

23. Kelly, M., "All their Eggs in One Basket: Portfolio Diversification of US Households," *Journal of Economic Behaviour and Organization* 27, 1995, pp. 87–96.

24. Merton, R. C., "Lifetime Portfolio Selection under Uncertainty: The Continuous-Time Case," *The Review of Economics and Statistics* 51, 1969, pp. 247–257; Merton, R. C., "An Analytic Derivation of the Efficient Portfolio Frontier," *The Journal of Financial and Quantitative Analysis* 7, 1972, pp. 1851–1872; Merton, R. C., "An Intertemporal Capital Asset Pricing Model," *Econometrica* 41, 1973, pp. 867–887.

25. Campbell, J.Y., & Viceira, L.M., *Strategic Asset Allocation: Portfolio Choice for Long-Term Investors*, Oxford University Press Inc., New York, 1st Edition, 2002.

26. Short selling refers to trading assets that are not owned.

27. Britten-Jones, M., Sampling Error in Mean-Variance Efficient Portfolio Weights, *Journal of Finance*, 1999, 12 pages.

C H A P T E R

METHODOLOGY AND DATA ANALYSIS

INTRODUCTION TO THE DATA

This chapter addresses opportunities for investors with high disposable income by analyzing the historical performance of 3 different asset classes: Fine Wine, Equities and Government bonds, and Equities and Treasury Bonds; and compares the financial performance of the Fine Wine 50 Index (FW50) to the FTSE 100 Index (FTSE100), the Dow Jones Industrial Average (DJIA), the UK Government Bonds Index (FTGB) and US 30 Year Treasury Bonds.[1]

Next, setting side-by-side portfolios consisting of Fine Wine, equities and bonds with portfolios consisting of equities and bonds determines the effects of holding Fine Wine. Data for a risk free rate (3-month London Inter-Bank Offer Rate[2] (LIBOR) and the 3-month US Euro/Dollar Deposit Rate) has been compiled by converting annual risk free rates to average monthly rates to enable the use of the prevailing risk free rate for the appropriate observation period.

The analysis focuses on 21 years of data in the form of monthly returns, from January 1983 to December 2003, and calculates nominal monthly returns from the change in movements in the monthly indices. The data frequency of the indices is monthly using month-end figures. Bloomberg, DataStream and the Financial Times were used to compile the financial indices.

The study is framed in 5-year observation periods on a rolling or moving average basis for each 12-month period. The first observation period is from 1983 to 1987, the next 1984 to 1998, and so on, ending in final 5-year observation period from 1999 to 2003. In addition, the data over the 10-year periods from 1983 to 1992, from 1993 to 2002, and from 1994 to 2003; over the 20-year periods from 1983 to 2002 and from 1984 to 2003; and over the 21-year period from 1983 to 2003 is examined.

Calculating the Returns on Alternative Investments

There are three basic methods for calculating returns on alternative investments. The first method is to create a composite index, based on data that varies over time or on fixed data. Varying indices can be chosen at random, as Goetzmann (1996)[3] does with paintings. For fixed indices the author often makes the selection. Kane (1984)[4] for example creates a hypothetical coin portfolio and records their prices at monthly intervals. Alternatively, the index can be chosen by experts, for example Burton and Jacobsen (2001)[5] follow the recommendations of two wine experts Parker (1985)[6] and Sokolin (1987).[7] Rush (1961)[8] and Frey and Serna (1990)[9] assessed returns on art collections where original purchase prices and dates were known. The drawback to the varying data index is that since different alternative investments come up for sale at different times, the index creator must be relied on to perform some sort of quality assessment for the index at each point in time. The fixed index, irrespective of how it is selected, avoids the potential drawback of varying quality over time; nonetheless its drawback is that it may become non-representative of the current state of the market if it contains increasingly unfashionable items. Eliminating certain vintages and adding others addresses this drawback.

The second method is to run a regression in which the price of an item is regressed on its various characteristics, including age or purchase price. This method allows one to estimate the price gain over the period attributable solely to this characteristic. This approach has the advantage of allowing for quality differences in the various collectibles within the index.

The third method is to collect data from repeat sales and run a repeat-sale regression, a technique first advanced by Bailey et al. (1963)[10] as an effective means for generating price indices for the real estate market. A repeat sale occurs whenever an identical asset is sold on 2 different occasions. A first growth producer makes anywhere between 15,000 and 20,000 cases of the same wine in a given vintage,[11] all of which can be regarded as multiples of one work, very much like paintings and prints. Compared to composite indices with varying data, this method generates a unique estimate as well as a standard error for each value of a log-price index, which can then be used to calculate the rate of price appreciation for the asset, and requires no adjustment for quality differences. Compared to the second approach, this method allows returns to vary over the sub-periods of a full time period. Nonetheless, this method has the drawback of selecting only those items that sell at least twice during the sample period, a shortcoming the second method addresses.

The choice between these methods depends to some extent on the type of alternative investment and the availability of data, in particular the similarity of the assets offered for sale and the frequency with which they come to auction. For example, in the wine and art market, many similar bottles or prints come up for sale frequently.

THE FINE WINE 50 INDEX

Indices are benchmarks used to monitor markets, assess performance and show the extent of wealth creation. Equity market indices, such as the MSCI, DJIA, S&P 500, FTSE 100, and commodity market indices, such as the Bordeaux Index, Fine Wine Index and the All Art Index, tend to be best known. Indices support asset allocation and diversification decisions, and risk measurement and management, as demonstrated in this study.

To quantify the risk-return characteristics of Fine Wine, an estimation of an index of Fine Wine prices is essential. Prices of blue chip investment grade wines tend to move closely together and therefore are best approximated by a single Fine Wine Index.[12] The Wine Price File,[13] an annual publication of some 90,000 wine prices sold at auction and retail is used to create the index, using the higher price from the high-low auction price. Prices are inclusive of buyer's premium. Data not included in the Wine Price File was obtained directly from Christie's and Sotheby's auction price catalogues. The earliest vintage in the index is 1961, thereby minimising the time-varying factor of the antique effect, which serves to distort the fundamental monetary return to wine. It also makes the simple assumption that all sales occur at the end of each period is adopted. The index also excludes charity auction results since emotion and the tax-deductibility of one's purchase price usually influences the bidding.

This book builds as its base a Fine Wine 50 Index.[14] The Fine Wine 50 Index is a composite index founded on data that varies over time, consisting of a basket of the same 10 Châteaux with 5 rolling vintages. At each point in time the index consists of 50 blue chip investment grade wines. Reputable Fine Wine experts and fund managers recommended the vintages and Châteaux that make up the index[15]. The Fine Wine 50 Index comprises blue chip investment grade wines that are most widely held and actively traded. The components of the FTSE 100 Index and the Dow Jones Index change over time; in the same way, the vintages change over time in the Fine Wine 50 Index. The index also maintains the same 10 Châteaux throughout. The Fine Wine 50 Index is based on a current widely-acknowledged and accepted Fine Wine Index,[16] which frequently features in financial and non-financial press including the Financial Times, the Oxford Companion to Wine[17] and wine journals alike.

The Fine Wine 50 Index measures total monthly return. Investment returns comprise income plus capital gains or losses, excluding either income or capital results in serious bias when measuring long-term returns. It must be noted that while short-term equity performance is driven by capital appreciation, long-term returns are driven by reinvested income,[18] therefore the Fine Wine 50 Index is compared to the FTSE 100 Index with Income Reinvested (data only available from 1993 to 2002), enabling a more accurate and reliable measure of long-term performance.

The Index comprises 50 cases of investment grade wine, made up of the same 10 Châteaux and 5 specific vintages for each observation period (shown in Appendix 2). The vintage years range from 1961 to 1990, and the selection of these Châteaux and vintages is based on historical performance and expert opinion.[19] Monthly price data for each of the 10 Châteaux and 5 vintages is collected from December 1982 to December 2003; and for each 12-month period, from 1983 to 2003, 5 specific vintages are selected and priced for each Château. This results in a monthly dataset consisting of 50 prices. The monthly prices for each Château and vintage are totalled to give a single total monthly price for all 50 cases of wine. This is repeated for each 12-month period using the same Châteaux but using different vintages (as shown in Appendix 2). The purpose of rolling forward vintages is to include the most profitable vintages and eliminate those that are no longer available or delivering significant returns.

The total monthly price data forms the basis to create the Fine Wine 50 Index taking December 1982 as the base month and assigning an initial value of its total price of '100.' Constructing the Fine Wine 50 Index is relatively simple, and involves a process of averaging and weighting. The underlying principle is that the percentage change in the index represents the change in value of the market. The index calculates the total price of all 50 cases and determines the percentage increase or decrease from the total of the previous month. Any percentage increase or decrease is reflected in the index and adjusted accordingly.

The returns calculated from the Fine Wine 50 Index, FTSE 100 Index, Dow Jones Index, FT Government Bonds Index and US 30 Year Treasury Bond Index are not net of transaction costs, the usual practice in such comparisons.[20]

OPTIMAL PORTFOLIO AND ASSET ALLOCATION METHODOLOGY

The objective in finding the optimal portfolio is to find the optimal weights for each asset class. When calculating the risk and return of a portfolio, the objective of an investor is to minimize the level of risk given a certain level of portfolio expected return. The methodology[21] used to calculate the efficient frontier and optimal portfolio is as follows:

Step 1
Step 1 converts the prices and index numbers into returns for each index. The data frequency of the indices is monthly and measured in pound sterling.

Step 2
Next, summary statistics of the individual returns for each index are calculated. The expected return is calculated as the arithmetic mean using 60 monthly returns. The risk of the monthly returns is calculated as the variance or standard deviation (the standard deviation is the square root of the variance). The covariance between FW50 and FTSE100/DJIA, between FW50 and FTGB/USGB, between FTSE100 and FTGB, and between DJIA and USGB is then calculated. A symmetric variance-covariance matrix is created, which shows the variance in its diagonal and the covariance in the off diagonal elements. Multiplying by 12, or respectively by 12, annualizes monthly-expected return and standard deviation figures.

Step 3

The methodology for calculating the portfolio return and portfolio variance is as follows: this phase sets up the weights for each asset class in the spreadsheet together with the function, which calculates the sum of the individual asset weights. The portfolio expected return and portfolio variance is calculated using the Multiplier function, the matrix multiplication command, in Excel. The portfolio standard deviation is the square root of the portfolio variance.

Step 4

The objective now is to minimize the portfolio variance by allowing the weights to change, subject to a number of constraints. By inputting the required rate of return, the Solver function is used to minimize the portfolio variance. The portfolio variance that needs minimising is selected. Constraints are then selected; portfolio return should be equal to a constant; the sum of all the asset weights should be equal to one; and the individual asset weights should be greater than or equal to zero (and not greater than one implying no short selling).

Step 5

This process is repeated a number of times using Solver for different values of portfolio expected return (the constraint). Minimizing the portfolio variance subject to different values for the expected portfolio return generates different points on the efficient frontier.

Step 6

The points generated in Step 5 are used to produce the graph of the efficient frontier. To graph the efficient frontier, 2 columns are created, one, which contains the portfolio standard deviation (x-variable) and the portfolio expected return (y-variable). An XY-scatter diagram is chosen to graph the values. A graph for the efficient frontier (the portfolio expected return on the y-axis and the portfolio standard deviation on the x-axis) is created for each 5, 10 and 20-year period.

Step 7

A second y-variable, the transformation line, has an intercept equal to the risk free rate (UK – 3-month LIBOR, US – 3-month Euro/Dollar Deposit Rate) is drawn tangential to the highest point with the efficient frontier to produce the Capital Market Line (CML). The optimal portfolio, the point where the CML is at a tangent to the efficient frontier determines the optimal weights held in each asset class, the portfolio expected return and portfolio standard deviation or risk.

Step 8

The Sharpe ratio, which measures portfolio performance in terms of its risk-adjusted return (excess return to standard deviation), is calculated for each observation period. The risk premium is calculated by subtracting the 3-month LIBOR/3 month Euro/Dollar Deposit Rate from portfolio expected returns. For each observation period the correlation coefficient between the indices and beta is calculated. A CAPM expected return is compared to the historic expected return given by the Fine Wine 50 Index, to determine whether or not to invest in Fine Wines. The FTSE 100 Index and the Dow Jones Index serves as a proxy for the market portfolio respectively.

Step 9

This process is repeated for each 5, 10 and 20-year period. The process is also repeated for a portfolio consisting of Equities and Government Bonds only, and for portfolios consisting of Equities with Income Reinvested for UK data only. This analysis is carried out in 5-year, 10-year and 20-year observation periods from January 1993 to December 2002,[22] a 20-year observation period from January 1984 to December 2003, and a 21-year observation period from January 1983 to December 2003 have therefore been included in the analysis.

ENDNOTES

1. The FTSE 100 Index, the Dow Jones Index, the UK Government Bonds Index and the US 30 Year Treasury Bonds Index are portfolios with systematic risk not idiosyncratic risk.
2. 3-month LIBOR and the 3-month Euro/Dollar Deposit Rate is a benchmark and changes constantly under the direct influence of supply and demand.
3. Goetzmann, W.N. "How Costly is the Fall from Fashion? Survivorship Bias in the Painting Market." *Economics of the Arts—Selected Essays*, 1996, pp. 71–84.
4. Kane, A. "Coins: Anatomy of a Fad Asset." *Journal of Portfolio Management* 1:2, 1984, pp. 44–51.
5. Burton, B.J., & Jacobsen, J.P. "The Rate of Return on Investment in Wine." *Economic Inquiry* 39, 2001, pp. 337–350.
6. Parker, R. *Bordeaux: The Definitive Guide for the Wines Produced since 1961*. New York: Simon & Schuster, 1st Edition, 1985.
7. Sokolin, W. *Liquid Assets*. New York: Macmillan, 1st Edition, 1987.
8. Rush, R.H. *Art as an Investment*. New Jersey: Prentice-Hall, 1st Edition, 1961.
9. Frey, B.S., & Serna, A. "Der Preis der Kunst." *Kursbuch* 99, 1990, pp. 105–113.
10. Bailey, M., Muth, R., & Nourse. "A Regression Method for Real Estate Price Index Construction." *Journal of the American Statistical Association* 58, 1963, pp. 933–942.
11. Fine Wine Management Limited.
12. Burton, B.J., & Jacobsen, J.P. "The Rate of Return on Investment in Wine." *Economic Inquiry* 39, 2001, pp. 337–350.
13. Edgerton, W. *Edgerton's Wine Price File*. Wine Technologies Inc., United States, 16th Edition, 2002.
14. The Fine Wine 50 Index is as robust as the FTSE 100 Index and the FT Government Bonds Index.
15. Fine Wine Management Limited, OWC Asset Management, Premier Cru Fine Wine Investment Ltd.
16. Fine Wine Management Ltd.
17. Robinson, J. *The Oxford Companion To Wine*. New York: Oxford University Press Inc, 2nd Edition, 1999.
18. Pickford, J. *Financial Times Mastering Investment*. London: Prentice-Hall, 1st Edition, 2002.
19. Parker, R. *Bordeaux: The Definitive Guide for the Wines Produced since 1961*. New York: Simon & Schuster, 1st Edition, 1985. Sokolin, W. *Liquid Assets*. New York: Macmillan, 1st Edition, 1987.
20. Burton, B.J., & Jacobsen, J.P. "The Rate of Return on Investment in Wine." *Economic Inquiry* 39, 2001, pp. 337–350.
21. Cuthbertson, K., & Nitzsche. *Investments: Spot & Derivatives Markets*. Sussex: John Wiley & Sons Ltd, 1st Edition, 2001.
22. Only 10 years of data available for Income Reinvested.

C H A P T E R

CRITICAL EVALUATION AND INTERPRETATION OF RESULTS

EXPECTED RETURN, STANDARD DEVIATION AND COMPOUND GROWTH RESULTS

O ver the 20-year period from 1983 to 2002, the expected return[1] on the Fine Wine 50 Index (12.3% p.a.) exceeds that on (1) the FTSE 100 Index (9.2% p.a.) and the UK Government Bonds Index (1.2% p.a.) and likewise for (2) the Dow Jones Index (11.7%) and the US 30 Year Treasury Bonds ((0.3% p.a.)). The reason behind the negative returns on the US 30 Year Treasury Bonds lies behind the fact the 80's in the US enjoyed a period of economic boom and a sustained period of high interest rates peaking at 15%, and so the bond yields during this period were high. Over the past 20 years interest rates have fallen to significantly low levels and as a result bond yields have fallen significantly. Thus, over the 20 year period from 1983 to 2002 bond yields have fallen significantly compared to equity returns. The Fine Wine 50 Index (13.9% p.a.) has a lower volatility as measured by its standard deviation[2] than (1) the FTSE 100 Index (16.5%) but a higher volatility than the UK Government Bonds Index (6.2% p.a.); likewise for (2) the Dow Jones Index (15.9% p.a.) and the US 30 Year Treasury Bonds Index (1.1% p.a.). The compound growth rate[3] of the Fine Wine 50 Index (11.4% p.a.) exceeds that of (1) the FTSE

100 Index (7.6% p.a.) and the UK Government Bonds Index (1.2% p.a.) and likewise for (2) the Dow Jones Index (10.3% p.a.) and the US 30 Year Treasury Bonds Index ((4.2% p.a.).

Incorporating 2003 data gives a similar pattern of results for the FTSE 100 Index and UK Government Bonds Index over the 20-year period from 1984 to 2003. The same is true over the 21-year period from 1983 to 2003. This result is not the case for the Dow Jones Index. Over the 20-year period from 1984 to 2003 the expected return for the Dow Jones Index exceeds the Fine Wine 50 Index by 0.4% p.a. and by 0.5% p.a. over the 21-year period from 1983 to 2003. In 2003 the US enjoyed strong economic growth, greater investor confidence, recovery in the financial markets and low interest rates, whereas the rate of recovery in the UK has been a lot slower (find the complete set of expected return results in Appendix 18). The standard deviation results for the 20-year period from 1984 to 2003 and for the 21-year period from 1983 to 2003 follow the same pattern of results as the 20-year period from 1983 to 2002 for both the UK and US indices (find the complete set of standard deviation results in Appendix 19). As expected, the compound growth rate results for the 20-year period from 1984 to 2003 and for the 21-year period from 1983 to 2003 follow the same pattern of results as the 20-year period from 1983 to 2002 for the FTSE 100 Index. The compound growth rate for the Dow Jones Index over the 20-year period from 1984 to 2003 exceeds the Fine Wine 50 Index by 0.4% p.a. and is equal to that of the Fine Wine 50 Index over the 21-year period from 1983 to 2003 (find the complete set of compound growth rate results in Appendix 20).

Over the 10-year period from 1993 to 2002, the expected return and standard deviation of the Fine Wine 50 Index (15.0% p.a. and 15.9% respectively) exceeds that for the 10-year period from 1983 to 1992 (9.5% p.a. and 11.5%). In contrast both the FTSE 100 Index and the Dow Jones Index performed better in the earlier 10-year period achieving an expected return of 14.1% p.a. for the FTSE 100 Index and

12.8% for the Dow Jones Index compared to 4.3% p.a. for the FTSE 100 Index and 10.6% p.a. for the Dow Jones Index in the 10-year period from 1993 to 2002. The same pattern of results exists when 2003 data is added. Over the latter 10-year period the FTSE 100 Index (IR) achieved an expected return of 7.9% p.a. One would expect the return to be higher for a corresponding index with income reinvested (find the complete set of the expected return and standard deviation results for both the UK & US indices for all summary observation periods in Appendix 18 and 19).

The earlier boom periods of the bull market, when the economic activity of the 80's and early 90's, favored equity investment. The investment market for Fine Wine was an emerging market in the 1980s. Nonetheless, the Fine Wine 50 Index achieved good returns with relatively low volatility compared to the FTSE 100 Index and Dow Jones Index.

The Fine Wine 50 Index delivered superior returns (peaking at 27.1% p.a. in the 5-year period from 1993 to 1997) in the 90's and in the early 80's. These periods of high returns coincided with the release of great vintages (1982, 1985, 1986, 1989 and 1990), creating high levels of demand and trading activity in Fine Wine.

The returns to Fine Wine increase significantly with the release of a great vintage. In the late 80's Fine Wine continued to deliver good returns, but these were not as high as the returns to traditional financial assets in the early 80's and early 90's. Also high interest rates during these specific periods in both the UK & US encouraged households to save more as bank deposits.

Equities supply good returns consistently throughout the 80's and 90's, with the exception of the 5-year period from 1990 to 1994, which coincided with the 1990-1992 recession. The FTSE 100 Index achieved low returns in the 5-year period from 1997 to 2001 and negative returns in the 5-year period from 1998 to 2002, unlike the Dow Jones Index, due primarily to the global economic slowdown and volatile financial markets since 2001. The US economy is more resilient to such shockwaves. The Fine Wine 50 Index continues to perform well since the recent collapse of the bull.

Fine Wine investment tends to be affected only by global recession and global economic downturn. It's clear from the results that the expected return for the 5-year period from 1998 to 2002 reached its lowest point of 3% p.a. Despite this low return, Fine Wine still outperformed equities ((4%) p.a. for FTSE 100 Index and 2.9% p.a. for the Dow Jones Index) in this boom and bust period. The conclusion to drawn from all this is that Fine Wine investment is less volatile than equity investment over the long term, but tends to be more volatile in the short term, supporting the case that investors hold Fine Wine for a minimum of 5 years in order to realize significant returns from this investment.

CORRELATION COEFFICIENT RESULTS

The riskiness of a portfolio of 2 assets depends on the sign and size of the correlation coefficient. For most investments correlation coefficients tend to lie between 0 and +1, because general economic changes (interest rates, inflation and exchange rates) influence the returns on assets, to a greater or lesser extent, in similar ways. This is particularly true for the return on equities and bonds,[4] implying that risk reduction is possible through diversification, but the total elimination of risk is unlikely. If the correlation coefficient is +1, the returns for the 2 assets are perfectly positively related and the asset returns always move in the same direction, but not necessarily by the same percentage amount. In this case, the risk cannot be reduced through diversification. If the correlation is −1, the converse applies: portfolio risk can be eliminated through diversification. If the correlation coefficient is zero, the asset returns are not related, so risk can be reduced through diversification, but it will not be eliminated. So long as the correlation between returns is less than +1, there tends to be some diversification benefit, and overall portfolio risk is reduced.

Most investors would expect equity and bond returns to have a negative correlation or an inverse relationship, expecting them to move in completely opposite directions.[5] If an economy is weak or unstable this will inevitably impact company profitability, and the stock market. Simultaneously, this will cause interest rates to fall from lower inflationary pressures, and such a fall in interest rates results in capital gains in bonds at a time when there might be an occurring capital loss on equities.

Over the 20-year period from 1983 to 2002 the correlation coefficient[6] between (1) the FTSE 100 Index and the UK Government Bonds Index was +0.28; for the 10-year period from 1993 to 2002 it was +0.19 and (2) the Dow Jones Index and the US 30 Year Treasury Bonds Index was -0.11%. For the 20-year period from 1984 to 2003 the correlation coefficients were +0.27 and -0.07% respectively. Likewise for the 21-year period from 1983 to 2003 the correlation coefficients were 0.26% and -0.09% respectively. UK equity and bond returns have a correlation coefficient close to zero, implying a weak or negative relationship for the period 1983 to 1992 and for the period from 1997 to 2001; for the period from 1992 to 1996 they have a correlation coefficient less than 1 and greater than zero implying a strong or positive relationship.[7] Note that US equity and bond returns typically have lower correlation coefficients over the long term compared to corresponding UK equity and bond returns. This is very characteristic of the US market, given the continuous fall in interest rates to very low levels in recent years, coupled with double-digit equity returns in the 80's and 90's. Over the short term this relationship is reversed. (See Appendix 21 for the complete set of correlation coefficient results.)

So why do equity and bond returns move together, i.e. show positive correlations as demonstrated in these results? The 1990s were a classic example of a cycle of lower interest rates from falling inflation, thereby increasing equity returns. Falling interest rates meant a lower discount rate could be used to value the future cashflows of companies, combined with a corresponding increase in their valuations. In addition, company debt servicing costs fell, thereby increasing profitability levels. Due to falling yields, both the equity and bond markets experienced capital gains. In part, this may be what the markets have experienced recently. The difference this time is that the UK and the US are not in a period where inflation is rapidly falling. Periods of negative correlation between equity and bond returns have coincided with periods of stable inflation.[8]

An alternative interpretation is that investors' expectations in the equity market are different from those in the bond market, bond investors being more bearish about the economic outlook. If this is the case, then at some stage one market will be right, and the other wrong, and the joint movement in equity and bond returns will come to an end. Bonds are stable assets and tend to serve as hedge investments in periods of economic setbacks, as evidenced in the 1987 stock market crash when bond prices rose sharply. For example, in the 5-year period from 1998 to 2002, the correlation coefficient between the FTSE 100 Index and the UK Government Bonds Index was -0.17%. This negative correlation is a classic example of investors expecting equity and bond returns to have an inverse relationship. Investors are responding to the current global downturn by investing heavily in bonds and minimizing their exposure to the volatility of the stock market.

Over the 20-year period from 1983 to 2002 the correlation coefficient[9] between the Fine Wine 50 Index and (1) the FTSE 100 Index was +0.02 and (2) the Dow Jones Index was +0.03%. This result is the same for the 20-year period from 1984 to 2003 and for the 21-year period from 1983 to 2003. The correlation coefficient between the Fine Wine 50 Index and the FTSE 100 Index (IR) was +0.01 for the 10-year period from 1983 to 2002. Over the 20-year period from 1983 to 2002 the correlation coefficient between the Fine Wine 50 Index and (1) the UK

Government Bonds Index was zero and (2) the US 30 Year Treasury Bonds Index was +0.05%. This result is the same for the UK Government Bonds Index for the 20-year period from 1984 to 2003 and for the 21-year period from 1983 to 2003. For the US 30 Year Treasury Bonds Index this result is +0.03% for both periods. The correlation coefficient results of the UK and US indices with the Fine Wine 50 Index are very similar.

The correlation coefficients between Fine Wine and equities, and between Fine Wine and government bonds, display similar characteristics over almost all periods from 1983 to 2003, having either no relationship with a correlation close to zero or a weak negative relationship with a correlation less than 0. The returns to Fine Wine are generally unaffected by movements in the financial markets, whether equities or bonds. Fine Wine therefore serves as an effective hedge asset against traditional financial assets. In fact Fine Wine serves as a better hedge than bonds, because of this low or negative correlation, despite Fine Wine being more volatile than bonds.

A good hedge asset has a negative correlation with other assets in the portfolio, and such assets are particularly effective in reducing overall portfolio risk. Investors prefer to add to their portfolios assets with low, or even better, negative correlations.[10] While a portfolio's expected return is the weighted average of its component expected returns, its standard deviation is however less than the weighted average of the component standard deviations because of diversification benefits. Portfolios of less than perfectly correlated assets always offer better risk-return opportunities than the individual component assets on their own; the lower the correlation between the assets, the greater the gain there is in efficiency. When the correlation coefficient is −1, it's possible to obtain a perfectly hedged position. At best the correlation coefficient between Fine Wine and equities or bonds in this study over the 20-year period is negative 0.2, offering some diversification benefit and implying that

risk can be reduced through diversification but cannot be eliminated. Potential benefits from diversification arise when correlations are less than perfectly positive (less than +1).

Combining different types of asset classes that do not move
together "is one of the very few instances in which there is a free
lunch—you get something for nothing."[11] The right combination of
assets can reduce the volatility of an asset portfolio, without reducing
the expected return over time. Financial assets like equities and bonds
tend to respond to the same global economic conditions. Non-financial assets tend not to be affected by general economic conditions;
investors may therefore want to consider holding Fine Wine as part of
a diversified portfolio of financial assets, since holding it not only has
the potential to increase portfolio expected return but also bring about
significant diversification benefits that may reduce overall portfolio
risk.

OPTIMAL RISK-RETURN EFFICIENT PORTFOLIO RESULTS

Each risky portfolio on the efficient frontier consists of a number of
risky assets held in fixed proportions.[12] Introducing a risk free asset
generates the transformation line, which is a linear relationship between expected return and risk for a portfolio consisting of one safe
asset (3-month LIBOR[13] or 3-month Euro/Dollar Deposit Rate) plus
one risky portfolio (Fine Wine 50 Index and FTSE 100 Index or Fine
Wine Index and the Dow Jones Index). The transformation line has an
intercept equal to the risk free rate. Here the investor invests solely in
the safe asset where the standard deviation is zero. Investors place all
their wealth in a single asset class on the boundary points of the
efficient frontier.

In periods of high interest rates, like those experienced in the late 1980s and the early 1990s, it makes economic sense to hold safe assets, for instance, bank deposits that offer higher risk-free rates of return compared to equities.[14] The 5-year periods from 1986 to 1990, 1987 to 1991, 1988 to 1992, 1990 to 1994 and the more recent 5-year period from 1998 to 2002, suggest that an investment in the risk free rate (bank deposits) is preferred to an investment consisting of Fine Wine and/ or equities for UK indices. This result repeats for US indices, given the high level of interest rates in of the 80's and 90's. In these time periods the return on the risk free asset exceeds the expected return of the optimal risk-return efficient portfolio, and hence is the preferred investment.

The highest transformation line tangent to the efficient frontier provides the investor with the highest possible return per unit of risk. The highest possible transformation line tangential to the efficient frontier is the Capital Market Line. The point at tangency with the efficient frontier is the optimal risk-return efficient portfolio. The optimal risk-return efficient portfolio[15] using (1) UK indices and (2) US indices for the 20-year period from 1983 to 2002 has an expected return of (1) 12% p.a. and (2) 12% p.a. and a standard deviation (1) 12.7% p.a. and (2) 10.6% p.a. and consists of (1) 91% Fine Wine and 9% equities and (2) 58% Fine Wine and 42% equities. The maximum-return portfolio[16] for the same period is the same for UK and US indices, and has an expected return of 12.3% p.a. and a standard deviation of 13.9% p.a., and consists of 100% Fine Wine. The minimum-risk portfolio[17] for the same period has an expected return of (1) 3.6% p.a. and (2) 0% and a standard deviation of (1) 5.7% p.a. and (2) 1%, and consists of (1) 18% Fine Wine, 4% equities and 78% government bonds and (2) 1% Fine Wine, 1% equities and 98% treasury bonds. See Figure 5.1 for the UK results and Figure 10 for US results.

FIGURE 5.1

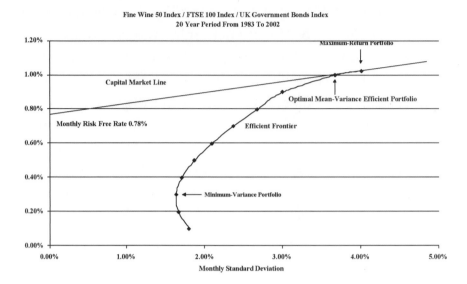

FIGURE 5.2

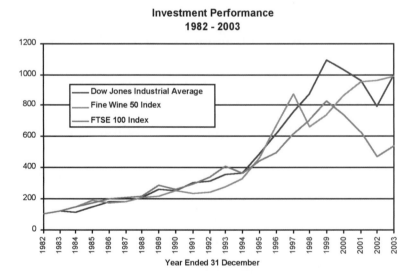

UK and US indices achieved similar results for the 20-year period from 1984 to 2003 and the 21-year period from 1983 to 2003. In the 21-year period, the optimal risk-return efficient portfolio for UK indices results in a 100% holding in Fine Wine and US indices resulting in a 91% holding in Fine Wine and 9% holding in equities. This is due primarily to the very turbulent nature of the financial markets and in particular the stock markets making a slow recovery after the 40% losses seen in the past few years. The Dow Jones performed better than the FTSE 100 Index and this has been demonstrated in the results. See Appendixes 22, 23, 24 and 25 for the complete set of results for optimal risk-return efficient, maximum return, and minimum risk portfolios. Figure 11 highlights the investment performance of the Fine Wine Index, FTSE 100 Index and the Dow Jones Index over the past 21 years rebased from 1982. Figure 12 shows a shorter and more recent investment horizon.

FIGURE 5.3

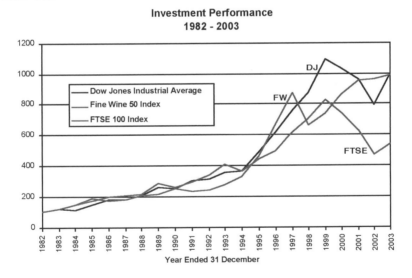

69

FIGURE 5.4

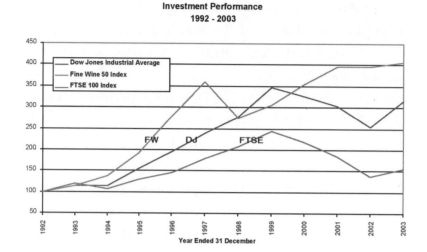

**Investment Performance
1992 - 2003**

The optimal risk-return efficient portfolio[18] using (1) UK indices and (2) US indices for the 10-year period from 1993 to 2002 has an expected return of (1) 15% p.a. and (2) 13.2% p.a. and a standard deviation of (1) 15.9% p.a. and (2) 11.5% p.a., and consists of (1) 100% Fine Wine and (2) 59% Fine Wine and 41% equities. The maximum-return portfolio[19] for the UK indices in the same period is identical to the optimal risk-return efficient portfolio. This suggests that the preferred optimal portfolio consisting solely of Fine Wine is highly efficient at trading off return against risk. The optimal risk-return efficient portfolio for the 10-year period from 1983 to 1992 has an expected return of (1) 14.1% p.a. and (2) 12% p.a. and a standard deviation of 18.4% p.a. and (2) 12.4% p.a., and consists of (1) 100% equities and (2) 26% Fine Wine and 74% equities. Again the maximum-return portfolio for the UK indices for this period is identical to the optimal risk-return efficient portfolio. The analysis demonstrates that portfolios consisting of equities with income reinvested produce a similar pattern of results. Nonetheless, in each 5-year period from 1993 to 2002 the weighting in equities with income reinvested is greater than the corresponding portfolios with equities without income reinvested. This reduces the weighting in Fine Wine in these periods, but does not change the underlying rationale or justification for holding Fine Wine in a diversified portfolio. Note that over the 5, 10, 20 or 21-year observation periods the US indices show a more balanced mix of Fine Wine and equities compared to the UK indices. This is due to the fact that over the long term the Dow Jones Index tends to be less volatile than the FTSE 100 Index coupled with the fact the Dow Jones Index has performed better in terms of expected returns than the FTSE 100 over the past 21 years.[20]

The percentage weighting held in UK Government Bonds and US 30 Year Treasury Bonds is minimal.[21] The weighting held in Fine Wine and equities, varies significantly over the 21 and 20-year period, the more recent 10-year period favoring Fine Wine and the earlier 10-year period favoring equities. Even so, UK portfolios for the 5-year periods from 1983 to 1987 and from 1984 to 1988 consisted of 63% and 35% Fine Wine respectively.[22] This period of growth and superior returns for the Fine Wine 50 Index is attributable to the release of the 1982 vintage. The 1987 stock market crash reduced investor confidence in equity investment and increased equity return volatility. It is clear from the UK and US results that the 1980s favored equity investment, with an increasing percentage weighting held in equities. Nonetheless, for this period in the late 1980s and early 1990s where both the UK and US experienced high interest rate levels, safe assets (3-month LIBOR or 3-month Euro/Dollar Deposit Rate) offered the highest rate of return.

The dominance of Fine Wine in the 1990s began in the 5-year period from 1990 to 1994. As far as the UK was concerned, the combination of what was seen as a high exchange rate and the persistence of high interest rates meant that the period of ERM membership coincided with the 1990-1992 recession. In the 1990s the world economy enjoyed a boom and optimism was high; hence the optimal risk-return efficient portfolios in the 1990s consisted of both Fine Wine and equities, with a greater percentage weighting in Fine

Wine than before. Interest rates were raised after mid-1999 until the end of 2000, as the combination of the oil price shock and a booming world economy threatened a rise in inflation. In 2001, interest rates were cut to avoid a recession, marking an end to the optimism about the rapid growth in future earnings of "new-economy" stocks. The post-2000 results, where the optimum risk-return efficient portfolio consisted of only Fine Wine for the 5-year periods from 1997 to 2001 and from 1998 to 2002, demonstrate this. The general cynicism of the time is further demonstrated in the optimal risk-return efficient portfolio analysis for equities and government bonds only, where the optimal portfolio for the 5-year period from 1998 to 2000 consisted of only government bonds.[23] The US indices show a similar pattern of results for these periods despite recovery in the US financial markets in 2003. This is reflected in the results for the 5-year period from 1999 to 2003 where a holding of 5% in US equities is preferred compared to 0% holding of UK equities in the same period.

The maximum-return portfolio[24] analysis demonstrates that the highest expected returns are achieved from investing in only Fine Wine or only equities for both the UK and US indices. For each 5-year period from 1983 to 1993 the maximum-return portfolios consist of only equities. In contrast for each 5-year period from 1990 to 2000 the maximum-return portfolios consist of only Fine Wine. In the case of portfolios consisting of the FTSE 100 Index (IR) the 5-year periods from 1995 to 1999 and from 1996 to 2000 consist of 100% equities achieving a marginally higher return and lower risk.[25] It is noted from the results that when 2003 data is added, over the long-term the maximum return portfolio consists of only equities, but equities still remain the most volatile asset class. It is clear from the results that holding single assets fail to deliver the diversification benefit of lower volatility. Holding more than one asset class in a well-diversified portfolio with a low or negative correlation between the assets may bring about significant diversification benefits with the effect of reducing overall portfolio risk.

The minimum-risk portfolio[26] analysis for each observation period demonstrates the significance of holding government or treasury bonds as part of a diversified portfolio of assets. Government bonds are stable assets, and because they have a lower correlation with Fine Wine than with equities, the analysis shows that most minimum-risk portfolios consist of Fine Wine and government bonds, with a much smaller weighting held in equities. Holding government bonds alone delivers a relatively low expected return peaking at c.4% in the UK. In contrast holding government bonds as part of a diversified portfolio with Fine Wine and equities, where the weighting in government bonds is high, the portfolio achieves a much higher expected return in most observation periods, peaking at 6% in the UK. These outlooks are due to the significant diversification benefits achieved by holding Fine Wine because of the low or negative correlation it has with equities and bonds. This is further demonstrated in the minimum-risk portfolio analysis[27] for equities and government bonds only, where the expected return is lower in the corresponding observation periods, peaking at 3.9% p.a. in the UK, which is equivalent to holding only government bonds. There are less diversification benefits from holding equities and government bonds because of the higher correlation between these assets. The US 30 Year Treasury Bonds have very low volatility and hence low expected returns. The minimum-risk portfolio results[28] show that for all observation periods a holding between 98% and 100% in treasury bonds is preferred. The main reason why this holding is greater in the US than in the UK is due to the lower level of interest rates and hence lower bond yields in the US.

SHARPE RATIO RESULTS

The market price for risk is given by $l_m = (ER_m - r) / s_m$. If every investor had the same expectations then l_m would be the same for all investors. However, in practice investors have different expectations, suggesting that this ratio may be different for each investor. This fails one of the assumptions of the CAPM, which states that investors have the same expectations, but also allows investors to use the Sharpe ratio[29] as a measure of relative the performance of different investment portfolios. If an investor holds any portfolio of assets composed of a subset of the assets of the market portfolio—in this case Fine Wine, equities and government bonds—then the Sharpe ratio is $S = (ER_p - r) / s_p$, where ER_p is the expected return of the portfolio, r is the risk free rate and s_p is portfolio standard deviation. Portfolios with higher Sharpe ratios have higher expected excess returns $(ER_p - r)$ per unit of risk (s_p) and are more effective in trading off return against risk.

In order to determine the effect Fine Wine has when held as part of a diversified portfolio of financial assets, the Sharpe ratio is calculated for all portfolios consisting of Fine Wine, equities and government bonds, and for all portfolios consisting of equities and government bonds only. This simple but highly effective comparison reveals the investment potential of Fine Wine, and clearly where the Sharpe ratio for diversified portfolios consisting of Fine Wine is higher than portfolios consisting of only financial assets, the benefits of holding Fine Wine becomes obvious: Holding Fine Wine as part of a diversified portfolio of financial assets, or held alone, makes good economic sense given its superior performance and significant diversification benefits.

For all observation periods from 1983 to 2002, portfolios consisting of Fine Wine have higher Sharpe ratios than portfolios consisting of equities and government bonds only.[30] Over the 20-year period from 1983 to 2002, the Sharpe ratio for a portfolio consisting of the Fine Wine 50 Index, FTSE 100 Index and UK Government Bonds is 0.06 compared to a Sharpe ratio of zero for a portfolio consisting of equities and bonds only. This same period achieves a higher Sharpe ratio result of 0.15 for a portfolio consisting of the Fine Wine 50 Index, Dow Jones Index and the US 30 Year Treasury Bonds. In fact, for the 20-year period from 1984 to 2003 and for the 21-year period from 1983 to 2003 there are strikingly similar results. For all observation periods the Sharpe ratio outcome for US indices are higher to those of the UK indices. This result highlights the strength of the Dow Jones Index over the FTSE 100 Index, and the Sharpe ratio result in particular demonstrates that US indices achieve higher expected returns per unit of risk compared to UK indices.

For the 10-year period from 1993 to 2002, a portfolio consisting of only Fine Wine has a higher Sharpe ratio of 0.14 compared to negative 0.06 for a portfolio consisting of equities only (FTSE 100 Index only),[31] showing that a portfolio consisting of only Fine Wine over this period outperforms a portfolio consisting of only equities. So not only does holding Fine Wine bring about significant diversification benefits, and reductions in overall portfolio risk, but also serves as an effective stand-alone investment that compares favorably to equity investment.

It is clear from the results that since the early 90's at a time when the investment market for Fine Wine attracted increased global investor interest, the Sharpe ratio continued to increase over the next 10 years, as interest rates continued to decline steadily in both the UK and US. Portfolios consisting of Fine Wine, equities and government bonds in the 5-year periods from 1991 to 1995, 1992 to 1996, 1995 to 1999, and from 1996 to 2000, had higher Sharpe ratios than portfolios consisting of only financial assets.[32] These effects are similar to those portfolios consisting of equities with income reinvested.

It is possible to have negative Sharpe ratios, signified by a downward sloping efficient frontier, that arise simply because the risk free rate is greater than the portfolio expected return. Negative Sharpe ratios appear for each 5-year period from 1986 to 1990, 1987 to 1991, 1988 to 1992, 1990 to 1994, and from 1998 to 2002.[33] A negative Sharpe ratio also arose over the 5-year period from 1998 to 2002 using US indices.[34] This result reversed when 2003 data was added, reflecting a recovery in both UK and US markets. The earlier 5-year periods in the late 1980s and early 1990s experienced periods of exceptionally high interest rates, hence the low or negative Sharpe ratios. The UK and the US both experienced a period of low asset returns and low interest rates in 2001 and 2002 due to the global economic slowdown and downturn in the financial markets.

BETA VALUE AND CAPITAL ASSET PRICING MODEL RESULTS

The beta and CAPM results provide additional analysis over and above the expected return, volatility, optimal portfolio and Sharpe ratio results consistent with Modern Portfolio Theory. The beta statistic compares the systematic risks of various assets. It is an index of the volatility of the individual asset relative to the volatility of the general market, and is calculated as the covariance of returns to (1) the Fine Wine 50 Index and the FTSE 100 Index divided by the variance of the returns to the FTSE 100 Index and (2) the Fine Wine 50 Index and the Dow Jones Index divided by the variance of the returns to the Dow Jones Index. The FTSE 100 and the Dow Jones Index is used as a proxy to the market and the risk premium is calculated as the difference between the expected return of (1) the FTSE 100 Index (market expected return) and 3-month LIBOR (risk free rate) and (2) the Dow Jones Index (market expected return) and 3-month Euro/Dollar Deposit Rate (risk free rate). The lower the beta, the less risk a particular asset is likely to contribute to a portfolio of assets. It is therefore a good strategy to include assets in a portfolio with low beta values.

Over the 20-year period from 1983 to 2002, the beta value[35] for (1) UK indices was 0.01 and (2) US indices 0.02. The beta values are at this low level for both the 20-year period from 1984 to 2003 and for the 21-year period from 1983 to 2003. For the 10- year period from 1993 to 2002, the beta value for (1) UK indices is 0.03 and (2) US indices 0.01, and for the 10-year period from 1983 to 1992 the beta value for (1) UK indices is 0.01 and (2) US indices 0.04. When the FTSE 100 Index (IR) is used as a proxy to the market the beta value is 0.01 for the 10-year period from 1993 to 2002. A beta value of 0.01 implies that Fine Wine returns are 99% less volatile than the market, and the market in this case is the FTSE 100 Index or the Dow Jones Index.[36] For each 5-year period from 1983 to 2002, betas are close to zero, peaking at 0.17 in the period from 1993 to 1997.[37] The near zero beta values arise simply because of the near zero correlation between (1) the Fine Wine 50 Index and the FTSE 100 Index and between (2) the Fine Wine 50 Index and the Dow Jones Index. The near zero beta values demonstrate the effectiveness of holding Fine Wine.

Note assets with beta values greater than 1 are expected to outperform the market, especially in a bull market. However, in a bear market these same assets are expected to fall by more than average. Assets with near zero beta values indicate that they are likely to be resistant to a bear market. Fine Wine returns are generally unaffected by economic and financial market movements especially when asset prices rise in a bull market. Fine Wine therefore serves as an effective hedge investment.

The Capital Asset Pricing Model (CAPM) implies that all correctly priced assets should lie on the Security Market Line. A key determinant of the required return is not the assets' variance but the assets' beta value. The CAPM expected return is calculated as the sum of the risk free rate plus beta multiplied by the difference between the markets expected return and the risk free rate. The market expected return in this case is the return on the FTSE 100 Index or the Dow Jones Index.

Over the 20-year period from 1983 to 2002, the 9.4% p.a. CAPM expected return is less than the 12.3% p.a. expected return for the Fine Wine 50 Index when the FTSE 100 Index is used as a proxy to the market.[38] This suggests that investors benefit from investing in the Fine Wine 50 Index, because the Fine Wine 50 Index gives a return c.31% greater than its contribution to overall portfolio risk.[39] Likewise, when the Dow Jones Index is used as a proxy to the market, over this same period, the 6.5% p.a. CAPM expected return is less than the

12.3% p.a. expected return for the Fine Wine 50 Index. This suggests that the Fine Wine 50 Index gives a return c.88% greater than its contribution to overall portfolio risk. CAPM results for the FTSE 100 Index and the Dow Jones Index remain fairly close to these results when 2003 data is added respectively. See Appendix 28 and 29 for the complete set of CAPM results.

Over the 10-year period from 1993 to 2002, the 7.2% p.a. CAPM expected return is less than the 15% p.a. expected return for the Fine Wine 50 Index when the FTSE 100 Index is used as a proxy to the market. This indicates that the Fine Wine 50 Index gives a return c.108% greater than its contribution to overall portfolio risk. In contrast for the 10-year period from 1983 to 1993, the 11.6% p.a. CAPM expected return is greater than the 9.5% p.a. expected return for the Fine Wine 50 Index again when the FTSE 100 Index is used a proxy to the market. Here, the Fine Wine 50 Index gives a return c.18% less than its contribution to overall portfolio risk. This result supports the findings that an investment in Fine Wine was a lot more profitable in the last ten years than in the 80's. When the Dow Jones Index is used as a proxy to the market, an investment in Fine was still a profitable investment in the 80's, but again, was much more profitable in the last 10 years (see Appendix 28 and 29).

As noted, over the 10-year period from 1993 to 2002 investors benefit from investing in the Fine Wine 50 Index since the Fine Wine 50 Index gives a return c.105% greater than its contribution to overall portfolio risk when the FTSE 100 (IR) Index is used as a proxy to the market. So even when equity indices with income reinvested are used the results are consistent with the findings that an investment in Fine Wine serves as an effective and profitable investment.

The results highlight the time periods when investors would benefit from investing in the Fine Wine 50 Index. For the 5-year periods from 1983 through to 1988, and from 1991 through to 2001, the Fine Wine 50 Index achieved an expected return greater than its contribution to overall portfolio risk, implying that investors benefit from an investment in the Fine Wine 50 Index. For all other 5-year periods the FW 50 Index achieved an expected return less than its contribution to overall portfolio risk, confirming that investors do not benefit from an investment in the Fine Wine 50 Index.

This pattern of CAPM results is completely consistent with the optimal risk-return efficient portfolio analysis,[40] which supports holding portfolios consisting of Fine Wine in the same time periods where the CAPM analysis[41] advocates investing in Fine Wine. Likewise the same is true for the periods where both the optimal risk-return efficient portfolio and CAPM analysis suggest not holding or investing in Fine Wine. This conclusion applies to both UK and US data over the past 21 years from 1983 to 2003.

UNDERLYING LOGIC BEHIND PORTFOLIO DIVERSIFICATION

The trade-off between risk and return implies that investors aim to maximize expected return on an asset portfolio while keeping the risk at a level that is consistent with their risk aversion. For an investor with a portfolio consisting of (1) the Fine Wine 50 Index and the FTSE 100 Index or (2) the Fine Wine Index and the FTSE 100 Index there is a trade off in terms of how much the expected return rises with an increase in the portfolio's standard deviation, i.e. extra risk.

In the case of a portfolio consisting of only the FTSE 100 Index, the trade-off expected return[42]/standard deviation[43] is 0.56 (= 9.2% / 16.5%) over the 20 year period from 1983 to 2002. For each percentage point increase in the standard deviation of the portfolio consisting of only the FTSE 100 Index, the investor is compensated with a 0.56% increase in expected return.

In the case of a portfolio consisting of only the Dow Jones 100 Index, the trade-off expected return/standard deviation is 0.74 (= 11.7% / 15.9%) over the 20 year period from 1983 to 2002. For each percentage point increase in the standard deviation of the portfolio consisting of only the Dow Jones Index, the investor is compensated with a 0.74% increase in expected return, 0.18% more than an investment in the FTSE 100 Index.

In the case of a portfolio consisting of only the Fine Wine 50 Index, the trade-off expected return / standard deviation is 0.88 (= 12.3% / 13.9%) over the 20 year period from 1983 to 2002. For each percentage point increase in the standard deviation of the portfolio consisting of only the Fine Wine 50 Index, the investor is compensated with a 0.88% increase in expected return, 0.14% more than an investment in the Dow Jones Index and 0.32% more than an investment in the FTSE 100 Index.

Therefore, there is a potential improvement in the trade-off between risk and return that comes from diversifying. If an investor holding a portfolio consisting of only the FTSE 100 Index is willing to add an investment in the Fine Wine 50 Index to the portfolio, this is likely to improve the risk-return trade-off, because the Fine Wine 50 Index trade-off is greater than the FTSE 100 Index trade off. Likewise if an investor holding a portfolio consisting of only the Dow Jones Index is willing to add an investment in the Fine Wine 50 Index to the portfolio, this is likely to improve the risk-return trade-off, because the Fine Wine 50 Index trade-off is greater than the Dow Jones Index trade off.

The effect of adding Fine Wine to the portfolio's expected excess return is simply the expected return of the Fine Wine 50 Index. The effect on the portfolio's variance is given by the correlation of the returns on the Fine Wine 50 Index and the returns on (1) the FTSE 100 Index and (2) the Dow Jones Index.[44]

Investors who hold portfolios consisting only of the FTSE 100 Index should add an investment in the Fine Wine 50 Index to their portfolio over the 20 year period from 1983 to 2002 if the ratio of Fine Wine 50 Index expected return[45] to standard deviation[46] divided by the correlation coefficient[47] between (1) the Fine Wine 50 Index and the FTSE 100 Index returns is greater than the ratio of the FTSE 100 Index expected return to its standard deviation and (2) the Fine Wine 50 Index and the Dow Jones Index returns is greater than the ratio of the Dow Jones Index expected return to its standard deviation. Therefore investors would benefit by adding Fine Wine to an Equity portfolio if:

(1) $((ER_{FW} / SD_{FW}) / r_{FWFT}) > (ER_{FT} / SD_{FT})$
(1) FTSE 100 Index $((12.3\% / 13.9\%) / 0.02) = $ **44.2** exceeds $(9.2\% / 16.5\%) = $ **0.56**.

This Fine Wine 50 Index figure exceeds the FTSE 100 Index figure, proof that adding Fine Wine to a UK equity portfolio brings about significant diversification benefits. This is also true for the Dow Jones Index:

(2) $((ER_{FW} / SD_{FW}) / r_{FWDJ}) > (ER_{DJ} / SD_{DJ})$
(2) Dow Jones Index $((12.3\% / 13.9\%) / 0.03) = $ **29.5** exceeds $(11.7\% / 15.9\%) = $ **0.74**.

Again this Fine Wine 50 Index figure exceeds the Dow Jones Index figure, which means adding Fine Wine to a US equity portfolio would bring about significant diversification benefits.

Greater diversification benefits arise from adding a portfolio of Fine Wine to UK equities than to US equities: there is a lower correlation between Fine Wine and the FTSE 100 Index (0.02) compared to the correlation between Fine Wine and the Dow Jones Index (0.03). It is this low correlation between returns that generates a significant improvement in the risk-return trade-off. Investors holding a portfolio consisting only of (1) the FTSE 100 Index or (2) the Dow Jones Index can use this to generate a portfolio that has an optimal risk-return trade-off.

There are comparable results when 2003 data is added. Despite the recovery in the UK and US financial markets in 2003, the above diversification benefits from holding a portfolio of Fine Wine still stands strong, since investments in Fine Wine is generally unaffected by turbulent financial markets and downturns in the economy, but is only generally affected by a global recession, something that has not been encountered for years.

ENDNOTES

1. Appendix 3 and Appendix 18.
2. Appendix 4 and Appendix 19.
3. Appendix 5 and Appendix 20.
4. Bodie, Z., & Kane, A., & Marcus, A.J. *Investments*. New York: McGraw-Hill/ Irwin, 5th Edition, 2002.
5. Modern Portfolio Theory.
6. Appendix 6 and Appendix 21.
7. Appendix 6.
8. Credit Suisse First Boston 2002.
9. Appendix 6 and Appendix 21.
10. Modern Portfolio Theory.
11. Gary Greenbaum, President of Investment Counselors Greenbaum & Associates in Oradell, New Jersey in Damato, K. "Finding Funds That Zig When Blue Chips Zag." *The Wall Street Journal*, June 17, 1997.
12. Modern Portfolio Theory.
13. London Inter-Bank Offer Rate.
14. Appendix 8 and Appendix 23.
15. Appendix 7 and Appendix 22.
16. Appendix 9 and Appendix 24.
17. Appendix 10 and Appendix 25.
18. Appendix 7.
19. Appendix 9.
20. Appendix 18 and Appendix 19.
21. Appendix 22.
22. Appendix 7.
23. Appendix 7.
24. Appendix 9 and Appendix 24.
25. Appendix 9.
26. Appendix 10 and Appendix 25.
27. Appendix 13.
28. Appendix 25.
29. The Sharpe ratio is a type of performance index, which can be used to rank the relative success of different investment strategies.
30. Appendix 14.
31. Appendix 14.
32. Appendix 14.
33. Appendix 14.
34. Appendix 26.
35. Appendix 15 and Appendix 27.
36. The Capital Asset Pricing Model.
37. Appendix 15.
38. Appendix 16 and Appendix 28.
39. Appendix 17 and Appendix 29.

40. Appendix 7 and Appendix 22.
41. Appendix 16 and Appendix 28.
42. Appendix 18.
43. Appendix 19.
44. Modern Portfolio Theory.
45. Appendix 18.
46. Appendix 19.
47. Appendix 21.

C H A P T E R

RISK ASSESSMENT OF
FINE WINE INVESTMENT

"Return Is Only Half The Equation"
and RiskGrades™

Economists and academics contend that risk should be quantified as rigorously as returns. Having established in the previous chapter the principles of measuring risk by way of the variance-covariance method, this chapter introduces J.P. Morgan's RiskGrades™ methodology,[1] a simple and transparent method for calculating the risk of an asset portfolio. It is intended for use by individual investors and small financial institutions, and therefore highly applicable to my aims. The concept is based on the variance-covariance approach. RiskGrades™ measure the volatility of assets or asset portfolios as the scaled standard deviation of the returns, called the RiskGrades™ (RG) of an asset or portfolio.

A RiskGrade™ of a diversified portfolio is not equal to the sum of the parts of the portfolio, due to the portfolio's diversification. Risk is not constant. As markets become more or less volatile, portfolios will become more or less risky. RiskGrades™ are dynamic; they change over time, reflecting market conditions. Risk is uncertainty, and in financial markets, risk is measured in terms of volatility of returns. Historical, volatility of returns is used to forecast future volatility and, hence, future risk. Since investors have different risk preferences, RiskGrades™ help investors monitor exposure to market risk, and allow comparison between investments.

RiskGrades™ scale all asset return volatilities from 0 to more than 1000. A RiskGrade™ of 100 is equivalent to 20% annual risk. This is approximately equal to the standard deviation of returns on a market capitalisation weighted portfolio of international indices during normal market conditions.[2] The low volatility portfolio arises because of big global diversification benefits.

The analysis of Fine Wine, equity and bond returns in the previous Chapter is valid and robust, and core modern portfolio theory and portfolio diversification concepts substantiate the analysis. Quite simply the RiskGrades™ methodology provides an additional value added measure over and above the standard deviation and beta values. The "standard deviation" is a classic portfolio risk measure since Markowitz used it in 1952 to demonstrate the diversification effect of assets. The standard deviation is a statistical gauge of volatility that measures the dispersion from the arithmetic mean of any data series, for example, a time series of returns. If there is not much variation from the mean, the dispersion will be small indicating a low risk investment and vice versa. As a measure of volatility, standard deviation is similar to RiskGrades™. Nonetheless, RiskGrades™ are based on exponential weighting of historical data, making them more adaptive to current market conditions. Exponential weighting significantly improves forecasting accuracy and responsiveness in varying market conditions.

The beta statistic is an index of the individual asset's volatility relative to the volatility of the general market. The beta statistic can be used to compare the systematic risks of different assets; the higher the beta, the more risk a particular asset is likely to contribute to an asset portfolio. This said, the beta statistic is only a relative risk measure of how an asset is likely to move relative to an overall index, and gives no indication of the asset's unique volatility or the overall market's volatility. The beta statistic only measures incremental systematic risk for a well-diversified asset portfolio.

RiskGrades™ are easier to interpret and are more intuitive reference points than the standard deviation and beta. Risk free assets are expected to have a RiskGrade™ of 0; less risky assets have a RiskGrade™ between 0 and 100; normal stocks have a RiskGrade™ between 100 and 300; very risky stocks, for example, technology stocks, have a RiskGrade™ between 600 and 800; and IPO's have a RiskGrade™ of more than 800. A RiskGrade™ of 200 is two times more risky than a RiskGrade™ of 100.

As noted in Chapter 5, the Fine Wine 50 Index is less volatile compared to the FTSE 100 Index and the Dow Jones Index over the long term.[3] I would therefore expect the Fine Wine 50 Index to have a lower RiskGrade™ than the FTSE 100 Index and Dow Jones Index. Likewise, I would expect the Dow Jones Index to have a lower RiskGrade™ than the FTSE 100 Index, given that the Dow Jones Index has proven to be less volatile than the FTSE 100 Index over the long term.[4]

CALCULATING RISKGRADES™

The most important part of calculating a RiskGrade™ (RG) is estimating the volatility or standard deviation of returns (Appendix 4). The RG of a single asset is simply the scaled daily or monthly standard deviation using the $\div T$ – rule, relative to the 20% volatility baseline. The RG of asset $_i$ using daily returns = $((s_i * \div 252) / s_{base}) * 100$ or using monthly returns = $((s_i * \div 12) / s_{base}) * 100$, where s_i is the daily or monthly standard deviation of asset$_i$ and $s_{base} = 0.2$ (20%) the base volatility.[5]

The RiskGrade™ of a portfolio of assets (RG_p) applies the standard formula for portfolio variance and RG simply replaces s in the formula for portfolio variance.

$$RG^2_p = (W^2_1 * RG^2_1) + (W^2_2 * RG^2_2) + (2 * W_1 * W_2 * r_{12} * RG_1 * RG_2),$$

where W_1 is the proportion held in asset $_1$ and W_2 is the proportion held in asset $_2$, and r_{12} is the correlation coefficient between asset $_1$ and $_2$.

The un-diversified risk grade (URG_p) of the portfolio is: $(W_1 * RG_1)$ + $(W_2 * RG_2)$. The diversification benefit (DB) is therefore equal to: Un-diversified risk grade (URG_p)—Portfolio RiskGrade™ (RG_p)

An additional concept that's intrinsic to determining RiskGrades™ is the marginal contribution to portfolio risk (the change in risk at a point in time as investors add or subtract one or more assets from the portfolio). This is called the percentage Risk Impact (% RI). The RI relates to a specific asset and reflects how the RG of an investor's portfolio would change if the investor were to sell that asset and keep the cash proceeds. The RI of asset $_i$ = RG of entire portfolio – RG of portfolio without asset $_i$. The % RI_i = (RI_i / RG of entire portfolio) * 100. When calculating the % RI it is assumed that when assets are excluded from the portfolio, they are sold for cash, and cash has a zero risk, s_{cash} = 0 and zero correlation with all other assets. The weight of the surviving assets will remain unchanged.

RiskGrades™ and its Application to Fine Wine Investment

To best demonstrate RiskGrade™ methodology, I use the 20-year period from 1983 to 2002 for the below equations. The complete set of results for (1) the 20-year period from 1983 to 2002, (2) the 20-year period from 1984 to 2003 and (3) the 21-year period from 1983 to 2003 are shown in Appendices 30, 31 and 32. In short, over these 3 periods the results are similar and consistent, and demonstrate that the RiskGrade™ of the Fine Wine 50 Index is less than that of both the FTSE 100 Index and the Dow Jones Index. Likewise, the RiskGrade™ of the Dow Jones Index is lower than that of the FTSE 100 Index.

Monthly volatility of return or standard deviation figures find the RiskGrade™ (RG) of the Fine Wine 50 Index, the FTSE 100 Index and the Dow Jones Index, where $RG = ((s_i * \div 12) / s_{base}) * 100$ and $s_{base} = 0.2$. The monthly standard deviation figures below are in decimals not percentages, i.e. $0.040068 = c.4.0\%$ for the Fine Wine 50 Index, $0.047704 = c.4.8\%$ for the FTSE 100 Index and $0.045994 = c.4.6\%$[6]. Over the 20 year period from 1983 to 2002:

(1) RiskGrade™ of the Fine Wine 50 Index =
   $((0.040068 * \div 12) / 0.2) * 100 = \mathbf{69.4}$
(2) RiskGrade™ of the FTSE 100 Index =
   $((0.047704 * \div 12) / 0.2) * 100 = \mathbf{82.6}$
(3) RiskGrade™ of the Dow Jones Index =
   $((0.045994 * \div 12) / 0.2) * 100 = \mathbf{79.7}$

As indicated earlier in the Chapter, and as expected, the Fine Wine 50 Index has a RiskGrade™ less than that of the FTSE 100 Index and less than that of the Dow Jones Index due to its lower volatility and its potential for maximum trade-off between risk and return (as demonstrated in the previous Chapter). These RiskGrade™ results are consistent with those results set out in Chapter 5. The Risk Grade of the FTSE 100 Index (82.6) and of the Dow Jones Index (79.7) is close to a RiskGrade™ of 100, as one would expect for a well-diversified equity portfolio.

The RiskGrade™ of a portfolio (RG_p) of Fine Wine and Equities is calculated using the formula:

$RG^2_p = (W^2_{FW} * RG^2_{FW}) + (W^2_{FT} * RG^2_{FT}) + (2 * W_{FW} * W_{FT} * r_{FWFT} * RG_{FW} * RG_{FT})$, where W_{FW} is the proportion held in Fine Wine 50 Index and W_{FT} is the proportion held in FTSE 100 Index, and r_{FWFT} is the correlation coefficient[7] between FW50 Index and FTSE 100 Index. For a portfolio holding 50% in the Fine Wine 50 Index and 50% in the FTSE 100 Index, the RG_p is equal to:

$RG^2_p = (0.5^2 * 69.4^2) + (0.5^2 * 82.6^2) + (2 * 0.5 * 0.5 * 0.01749 * 69.4 * 82.6)$
$= 2959.9$

$RG_p = \div 2959.9 = \mathbf{54.4}$

Similarly, a portfolio holding 50% in Fine Wine 50 Index and 50% in the Dow Jones Index, the RG_p is equal to:

$RG^2_p = (0.5^2 * 69.4^2) + (0.5^2 * 79.7^2) + (2 * 0.5 * 0.5 * 0.027701 * 69.4 * 79.7)$
$= 2867.1$

$RG_p = \div 2867.1 = \mathbf{53.5}$

As expected, the US equity and Fine Wine portfolio RiskGrade™ is less than that of the UK equity and Fine Wine portfolio RiskGrade™, the Dow Jones Index being less volatile than the FTSE 100 Index over the long term.

This RiskGrade™ represents the "diversified" RiskGrade™ of holding a portfolio of Fine Wine and Equities. The UK equity and Fine Wine portfolio RiskGrade™ (54.4) and the US equity and Fine Wine portfolio RiskGrade™ (53.5) is approximately 50% less risky than a well-diversified international all equity portfolio (RG of 100). These equity and Fine Wine portfolio RiskGrades™ of 54.4 and 53.5 respectively are less than the individual RiskGrades™ of holding only the Fine Wine 50 Index (69.4), holding only the FTSE 100 Index (82.6) and holding only the Dow Jones Index (79.7). This implies that there is a justification in holding both assets (Fine Wine and equities) as part of a diversified portfolio of assets.

The "un-diversified" RiskGrade™ (URG_p) is calculated using the formula:

$URG_p = (W_{FW} * RG_{FW}) + (W_{FT} * RG_{FT})$, where W_{FW} is the proportion held in Fine Wine 50 Index, RG_{FW} is the RiskGrade™ of the Fine Wine 50 Index. Over the 20-year period from 1983 to 2002, the URG_p of a portfolio holding the Fine Wine Index and the FTSE 100 Index is equal to $(0.5 * 69.4) + (0.5 * 82.6) = $ **76.0**

Likewise the URG_p of a portfolio holding the Fine Wine Index and the Dow Jones Index is equal to $(0.5 * 69.4) + (0.5 * 79.9) = $ **74.6**

Note that the un-diversified RiskGrade™ for the UK equity and Fine Wine portfolio (76.0) is lower than the RiskGrade™ of the FTSE 100 Index (82.6), implying that this un-diversified portfolio of Fine Wine and equities is less risky than an investment in the FTSE 100 only. Likewise, the un-diversified RiskGrade™ for the US equity and Fine Wine portfolio (74.6) is lower than the RiskGrade™ of the Dow Jones Index (79.7); this un-diversified portfolio of Fine Wine and equities is less risky than an investment in the Dow Jones Index only. The diversification benefit[8] (DB) is therefore equal to the un-diversified Risk Grade (URG_p) minus the diversified RiskGrade™ (RG_p). The FTSE 100 Index and Fine Wine 50 Index portfolio diversification benefit is equal to $76.0 - 54.4 = $ **21.6**, and thus risk is reduced by 21.6 RiskGrades™. The Dow Jones Index and Fine Wine 50 Index portfolio, the diversification benefit is equal to $74.6 - 53.5 = $ **21.1**, and thus risk is reduced by 21.1 RiskGrades™. Given that the actual correlation coefficient between the Fine Wine 50 Index and (1) the FTSE 100 Index and (2) the Dow Jones Index is less than +1, a portfolio equally weighted between Fine Wine and Equities drops risk substantially. The total risk reduction is equal to **28.4%** $= (21.6 / 76.0 * 100\%)$, for the FTSE 100 Index and Fine Wine 50 Index portfolio, and the risk reduction for the Dow Jones Index and Fine Wine 50 Index portfolio is equal to **28.3%** $= (21.1 / 74.6 * 100\%)$. These diversification benefits arise from the fact that Fine Wine and equities are not perfectly positively correlated. The diversification benefit reduces the portfolio's RiskGrade™ to a value that is less than the sum of the component RiskGrades™.

The diversification benefit varies according to the weights held in each asset class. A portfolio holding 75% in the Fine Wine 50 Index and

25% in the FTSE 100 Index over the 20-year period from 1983 to 2002 has a diversification benefit[9] (DB) of 16.4, which is less than that of an equally weighted portfolio (21.6), so in this case it makes economic and investment sense to hold 50% in Fine Wine (Fine Wine 50 Index) and 50% in equities (FTSE 100 Index). The calculation is as follows:

$RG^2_p = (0.75^2 * 69.4^2) + (0.25^2 * 82.6^2) + (2*0.75 *0.25 *0.01749 *69.4*82.6)$
$= 3173.2$
$RG_p = \div 3173.2 = \mathbf{56.3}$
$URG_p = (0.75 * 69.4) + (0.25 * 82.6) = \mathbf{72.7}$
$DB = 72.7 - 56.3 = \mathbf{16.4}$

Over the 20-year period from 1983 to 2002, for a portfolio holding 75% in the Fine Wine 50 Index and 25% in the Dow Jones Index, the diversification benefit[10] (DB) is 15.8, which is less than that of an equally weighted portfolio (21.1). Likewise in this case it makes economic and investment sense to hold 50% in Fine Wine (Fine Wine 50 Index) and 50% in equities (Dow Jones Index). The calculation is as follows:

$RG^2_p = (0.75^2 * 69.4^2) + (0.25^2 * 79.7^2) + (2*0.75 *0.25 *0.027701 *69.4*79.7)$
$= 3163.2$
$RG_p = \div 3163.2 = \mathbf{56.2}$
$URG_p = (0.75 * 69.4) + (0.25 * 79.7) = \mathbf{72.0}$
$DB = 72.0 - 56.2 = \mathbf{15.8}$

Over the 20-year period from 1983 to 2002, for a portfolio holding 25% in the Fine Wine 50 Index and 75% in the FTSE 100 Index, the diversification benefit[11] (DB) is 14.7, which is again less than that of an equally weighted portfolio (21.6). In this case it makes economic and investment sense to hold 50% in Fine Wine (Fine Wine 50 Index) and 50% in equities (FTSE 100 Index). The calculation is as follows:

$RG^2_p = (0.25^2 * 69.4^2) + (0.75^2 * 82.6^2) + (2*0.25*0.75*0.01749*69.4*82.6) = 4176.4$

$RG_p = \div 4176.4 = \mathbf{64.6}$

$URG_p = (0.25 * 69.4) + (0.75 * 82.6) = \mathbf{79.3}$

$DB = 79.3 - 64.6 = \mathbf{14.7}$

Over the 20-year period from 1983 to 2002, for a portfolio holding 25% in the Fine Wine 50 Index and 75% in the Dow Jones Index, the diversification benefit[12] (DB) is 14.4, which is again less than that of an equally weighted portfolio (21.1). In this case it makes economic and investment sense to hold 50% in Fine Wine (Fine Wine 50 Index) and 50% in equities (Dow Jones Index). The calculation is as follows:

$RG^2_p = (0.25^2 * 69.4^2) + (0.75^2 * 79.7^2) + (2*0.25*0.75*0.027701*69.4*79.7) = 3927.9$

$RG_p = \div 3927.9 = \mathbf{62.7}$

$URG_p = (0.25 * 69.4) + (0.75 * 79.7) = \mathbf{77.1}$

$DB = 77.1 - 62.7 = \mathbf{14.4}$

In terms of Risk Impact[13] (RI), on an absolute basis over the 20-year period from 1983 to 2002 an investment in the FTSE 100 Index is 82.6 / 69.4 = **1.2** times riskier than an investment in the Fine Wine 50 Index. An investment in the Dow Jones Index is 79.7 / 69.4 = **1.1** times riskier than an investment in the Fine Wine 50 Index. Staying with the equally weighted portfolio of Fine Wine and equities the RiskGrade™ of the FTSE 100 Index exceeds the RiskGrade™ of the Fine Wine 50 Index by **13.2** and the RiskGrade™ of the Dow Jones Index exceeds the RiskGrade™ of the Fine Wine 50 Index by **10.3**. It is assumed that a RiskGrade™ of 100 is equivalent to an annual volatility of 20%. Therefore, the FTSE 100 Index is more volatile than the Fine Wine 50 Index by an annual volatility of ((13.2 * 20%) / 100) = **2.6%**. Likewise the Dow Jones Index is more volatile than the Fine Wine 50 Index by an annual volatility of $((10.3 * 20\%) / 100) = \textbf{2.1\%}$. The diversification benefit reduces the portfolio's RiskGrade™ to a value that is less than the sum of the component RG's.

Staying with the equally weighted portfolio of the Fine Wine 50 Index and the FTSE 100 Index, over the 20-year period from 1983 to 2002, the Risk Impact (RI) value of the Fine Wine 50 Index is equal to:

RI_{FW} = RG of entire portfolio – RG of portfolio without Fine Wine and

$\% RI_{FW} = (RI_{FW} / RG$ of entire portfolio$) * 100$.

$RI_{FW} = 54.4 - (\div (0.5^2 * 82.6^2)) = 54.4 - 41.3 = \textbf{13.1}$

$\% RI_{FW} = ((13.1 / 54.4) * 100\%) = \textbf{24.1\%}$

This means that if an investor closes their Fine Wine 50 Index position, and sells their investment in the Fine Wine 50 Index for cash and keeps the cash proceeds, overall portfolio risk is reduced by 13.1 RiskGrades™ or 24.1%. The Risk Impact (RI) value of the FTSE 100 Index is equal to:

RI_{FT} = RG of entire portfolio – RG of portfolio without Equities and %

$RI_{FT} = (RI_{FT} / RG$ of entire portfolio$) * 100$.

$RI_{FT} = 54.4 - \sqrt{(0.5^2 * 69.4^2)} = 54.4 - 34.7 = \textbf{19.7}$

$\% RI_{FT} = ((19.7 / 54.4) * 100\%) = \textbf{36.2\%}$

This means that if an investor closes their FTSE 100 Index position and sells their investment in the FTSE 100 Index for cash and keeps the cash proceeds, overall portfolio risk is reduced by 19.7 RiskGrades™ or 36.2%. This, therefore, shows that the overall risk impact is greater or risk is reduced further if an investor reduces their weighting in the FTSE 100 Index. Reducing the weighting in the Fine Wine 50 Index has a smaller risk impact on the overall portfolio. Due to the diversification benefit that reduces portfolio risk, the sum of the Risk Impact values of the portfolio components for the Fine Wine 50 Index (24.1%) and FTSE 100 Index (36.2%) is less than 100% (= 60.3% (=24.1% +

36.2%)). This further strengthens the case to hold Fine Wine as part of a diversified portfolio of financial assets.

As in the above scenario, staying with the equally weighted portfolio of the Fine Wine 50 Index and the Dow Jones Index, over the 20-year period from 1983 to 2002, the Risk Impact (RI) value of the Fine Wine 50 Index is equal to:

RI_{FW} = RG of entire portfolio – RG of portfolio without Fine Wine and % RI_{FW} = (RI_{FW} / RG of entire portfolio) * 100.
RI_{FW} = 53.5 – (÷ (0.5^2 * 79.7^2)) = 53.5 – 39.8 = **13.7**
% RI_{FW} = ((13.7 / 53.5) * 100%) = **25.5%**

This means that if an investor closes their Fine Wine 50 Index position, and sells their investment in the Fine Wine 50 Index for cash and keeps the cash proceeds, overall portfolio risk is reduced by 13.7 RiskGrades™ or 25.5%. The Risk Impact (RI) value of the Dow Jones Index is equal to: RI_{FT} = RG of entire portfolio – RG of portfolio without Equities and % RI_{DJ} = (RI_{DJ} / RG of entire portfolio) * 100.

RI_{DJ} = 53.5 – (÷ (0.5^2 * 69.4^2)) = 53.5 – 34.7 = **18.8**
% RI_{DJ} = ((18.8 / 53.5) * 100%) = **35.1%**

This means that if an investor closes their Dow Jones Index position and sells their investment in the Dow Jones Index for cash and keeps the cash proceeds, overall portfolio risk is reduced by 18.8 RiskGrades™ or 35.1%; the overall risk impact is greater or risk is reduced further if an investor reduces their weighting in the Dow Jones Index. Reducing the weighting in the Fine Wine 50 Index has a smaller risk impact on the overall portfolio. Due to the risk-reducing diversification benefit, the sum of the Risk Impact values of the portfolio components, Fine Wine 50 Index (25.5%) and Dow Jones Index (35.1%) is less than 100% (= 60.6% (=25.5% + 35.1%), again strengthening the case of holding

Fine Wine as part of a portfolio of financial assets. In short holding a portfolio of Fine Wine as part of a portfolio of financial assets does bring about significant diversification benefits as demonstrated by the analysis in Chapter 5 and by this robust RiskGrades™ methodology. This said, there are still risks associated with investing in Fine Wine and holding a portfolio of Fine Wine.

RISKS ASSOCIATED WITH FINE WINE INVESTMENT

Fine Wine prices are subject to fluctuations and prices may fall as well as rise, even though historically Fine Wine prices tend to be less volatile than the financial markets. Fine Wine prices may decline to some extent in line with turbulent financial markets. An investment in Fine Wine is non-income producing in that it provides no interest or dividend income and capital return is wholly dependent on when one buys and sells the investment. Nor is the investment, at present, traded on any regulated, recognised exchange. Investment decisions and valuations are often based on the opinions of powerful wine critics.

Auction houses collect substantial commissions (whether buying or selling), and incidental costs reduce returns (as discussed in Chapter 2). Deciding on an exit point when capital is required may be difficult. Setting aside bottles of wine for 10-15 years goes against the "consume-it-as-you-go" culture. Spreads between bids and offers are wide, making it difficult for investors to make informed decisions about what to do with their stocks of Fine Wine. Buying wine futures also ties up funds for almost 2 years before the wine is delivered.

An investment in Fine Wine does attract additional transaction and incidental costs, for example, buying and selling commissions, shipping or transportation costs, storage or holding costs, and insurance. These costs may be difficult to quantify precisely at the outset, and if these costs are substantial, they may have an impact on the potential returns to Fine Wine. The Fine Wine investment market is smaller and less liquid than traditional financial investment markets. Still, it is recognised as a resilient store of wealth with significant tax advantages.

Poor harvests, possibly due to poor weather conditions, consequently decrease the demand for these vintages. But this may also increase the demand for other vintages. Fine Wine may deteriorate through poor storage and transportation conditions. A lack of proven provenance may have a significant negative impact on the price of wines; there have been a small number of isolated cases of counterfeit Fine Wine, in particular Châteaux Petrus and Châteaux Le Pin, which are believed to have originated in Switzerland.

Exposure to risk is minimized by buying the right wines, from the right vintages, at the right time, at a low cost, and selling the wine at high prices at the right time. Like most markets, hype, fashion and recommendation influences Fine Wine prices and the ability to make superior returns on investments. Successful Fine Wine collecting and investing requires knowledge, sound advice, timing, concentration on quality and provenance, and a genuine appreciation of Fine Wine. But invariably the biggest obstacle to making a significant return from trading wine is that the most prized bottles of wines, the wines that would bring the most money at auction, are the hardest ones to part with.

ENDNOTES

1. Berman, E. *Return is Only Half the Equation*. New York: The RiskMetrics Group, 1st Edition, 2000.
2. Actual volatility 18.85% over the 5 year period from January 1995 to December 1999.
3. Appendix 4 and Appendix 19.
4. Appendix 4 and Appendix 19.
5. Kim, J., Mina, J., Laubsch, A.J., & Lee, A. *RiskGrades^{TM} Technical Document*. New York: The RiskMetrics Group, 2nd Edition, 2000.
6. Appendix 19.
7. Appendix 21.
8. Appendix 30.
9. Appendix 31.
10. Appendix 31.
11. Appendix 32.
12. Appendix 32.
13. Appendix 30.

7

CONCLUSION, RECOMMENDATION, AND ADDITIONAL ALTERNATIVE INVESTMENT ISSUES

CHARACTERISTICS OF A GOOD INVESTMENT PORTFOLIO

In the United Kingdom an investment in Fine Wine is tax exempt. There are no penalties for early encashment. However, in the United States, the usual Capital Gains Tax may apply as with other collectibles. There are no dealing charges other than an auction's buying and/or selling commission. Moreover, some auction houses often waive either one of these commissions. Wine can be physically owned and enjoys global portability.

An investment in Fine Wine can offer superior returns, relatively low volatility that is separate from stock market volatility, and significant diversification benefits reducing overall portfolio risk (as noted in Chapter 5). The low or negative correlation between Fine Wine and financial assets makes Fine Wine an effective hedge investment. Investors are able to promote efficient diversification in the framework advanced by Markowitz (1952).[1] Great wines in great years constitute superior returns and almost any other combination yields at best below average returns.

There are seven characteristics of a good investment portfolio:[2]

Firstly, investment portfolios must not be too expensive to buy into, which is a key characteristic of the Fine Wine 50. This, therefore, eliminates those multi-million dollar minimum hedge funds.

Secondly, investment portfolios must offer superior returns. The Fine Wine 50 Index offered superior returns in the 1990s, unlike most money-market funds. On the other hand, this is also characteristic of the FTSE 100 Index and the Dow Jones Index.

Thirdly, investment portfolios ought to have low volatility. The RiskGrade™ for the Fine Wine 50 Index is less than that of the FTSE 100 Index and less than that of the Dow Jones Index (as noted in Chapter 6). This study demonstrates that a portfolio consisting of Fine Wine and equities has a lower volatility than one consisting of equities and bonds only.

Fourthly, investment portfolios must consist of assets that are either uncorrelated or negatively correlated with other assets and states of the economy. The Fine Wine 50 Index has a very low correlation with the FTSE 100 Index, the Dow Jones Index, the UK Government Bonds Index and with the US 30 Year Treasury Bonds Index, thereby offering significant diversification benefits.

Fifthly, investment portfolios should require very little active management and still deliver superior returns. Fine Wine can be held in storage at a cost for a number of years whilst appreciating in value as noted in Chapter 2, unlike those mutual funds that change direction whenever its manager changes.

Sixthly, investment portfolios should consist of assets that have low transaction and associated costs. Fine Wine does have additional transaction and incidental costs but these are often offset by substantial tax advantages or currency exchange fluctuations (as of 2005, the Euro has increased almost 40% against the US dollar in less than two years).

Finally, investment portfolios should be tax-free or at least tax efficient. Fine Wine investment is tax-exempt, offering significant cost savings as noted in Chapter 2; unlike traditional financial investments that often attract income and capital gains tax. In the United States, Capital Gains Taxes may apply subject to record keeping and the markets in which the wine is purchased and sold.

ADDITIONAL ALTERNATIVE INVESTMENT ISSUES

In this section, I include some supplementary topics that came up during the research and writing of this book, which, whilst being outside its primary focus, could, nonetheless, benefit from future investigation.

If diversified portfolios consisting of collectibles or Fine Wine provide a useful hedge against financial assets and inflation, some financial institutions may want to offer investment funds that invest in these items. Solomon Smith Barney created an alternative investment index in the 1980's. But generally financial institutions have stayed clear of creating investment funds dominated by these items.

Online auction sites, eBay.com for example, are creating a bank of data on alternative investments and prices. These auction sites typically have low transaction costs. And there is a high degree of control over bidding by both the seller and the buyer. The seller can specify the type of auction (English or Dutch), the minimum bid allowed, and length of time over which bids will be accepted, and a reserve price that is not revealed to the buyers. The buyer can specify the maximum acceptable bid and allow the site to increase bids automatically up to the maximum. Bid histories become available on-line after each auction closes, allowing investors to see both which items did not sell, and for those that did sell, what all the losing bids were as well as the winning bids. But as to whether on-line auctions are more market and information efficient compared to the traditional auction houses is a question that remains unanswered.

Auction data often gives a realistic feel for price appreciation. In some cases auction data often appears to be much more volatile than actual wine prices, thereby distorting them. Do Fine Wine price guides reflect the actual prices observed in actual trades? What difference would it make to price indices to go beyond auction house data and to use appraiser data, which may contain information from private or dealer transactions?

Prices used in the Fine Wine 50 Index are based on secondary market auction prices and not on primary market prices. The methodology may be repeated using these primary en primeur or release prices. Further research could be undertaken to determine whether buying into the Fine Wine 50 Index some time after the initial release price, that is when the price of a wine in the index has already risen, is something that an investor may want to do.

ENDNOTES

1. Markowitz, H.M. "Portfolio Selection." *Journal of Finance* 7, 1952, pp. 77–91.
2. From empirical analysis and from academic and non-academic literature (financial and otherwise).

APPENDIXES

APPENDIX 1
PRICE VARIATION OF THE 1982 FIRST GROWTHS SINCE RELEASE

The table below[1] shows the prices at which the 1982 Bordeaux First Growths were released and their selling prices in the 1990s. The prices of wines at release from this highly successful vintage were the same. Nonetheless, there are now considerable variations in the market's perception of quality, and hence, value.

Approximate Selling Price Per Case (£)			
	1983	Q4–1998	Q1–1999
Châteaux Haut-Brion	300	1,800	1,650
Châteaux Lafite-Rothschild	300	2,600	2,400
Châteaux Latour	300	2,900	2,750
Châteaux Margaux	300	2,800	2,650
Châteaux Mouton-Rothschild	300	3,400	3,200

Since 1995, opening prices for Bordeaux wines have increased significantly. Between 1994 and 1996 the release prices of the first growths rose from £395 per case to £995. The price increases between the two great vintages of 1995 and 1996 were significant. The 1995s are great wines priced relatively low, so they have good investment potential. The 1996s have relatively high prices an are not in the same league as the 1995s, Mouton-Rothschild being the exception. The good but not great 1997's prices were so out of sync with their inherent quality that it is difficult to see who, other than the primary producers, will ever make a return from them. To a certain extent, the proprietors are simply responding to the market forces of supply and demand, and increasing their prices as a result, but the perception of quality does not bring prices down in lesser years. Most proprietors released their 1997 vintage wines at higher prices than the 1996s, even though the quality is incomparably lower in most cases.

---

1. Extracted from Robinson, J. 1999 *The Oxford Companion To Wine*. New York: Oxford University Press Inc, 2nd Edition.

APPENDIX 2
COMPILATION OF FINE WINE 50 INDEX

The following Fine Wines were used to compile the Fine Wine 50 Index:

First Growth Investment Grade Wines
Official Classification of Medoc of 1855

- Château Haut-Brion, **Bordeaux, Premier Cru, Red, Graves**
- Château Lafite-Rothschild, **Bordeaux, Premier Cru, Red, Pauillac**
- Château Latour, Bordeaux, **Premier Cru, Red, Pauillac**
- Château Margaux, Bordeaux, **Premier Cru, Red, Margaux**
- Château Mouton-Rothschild (since 1973), **Bordeaux, Premier Cru, Pauillac**

First Growth Investment Grade Wines
Official Classification of St-Emillion of 1955

- Château Cheval Blanc, Bordeaux, **Premier Grand Cru, Red, St.-Emillion**

First Growth Investment Grade Wine
Official Classification of Graves of 1959

- Château La Mission-Haut-Brion, **Bordeaux, Cru Classe, Red, Graves**

Second Growth Investment Grade Wines
Official Classification of Medoc of 1855

- Château Cos D'Estournel, **Bordeaux, Deuxieme Cru, Red, St.-Estephe**
- Château Pichon Lalande, **Bordeaux, Deuxieme Cru, Red, Pauillac**

Investment Grade Wine
Unclassified

- Château Petrus, **Bordeaux, Red, Pomerol**

The Vintage Years used to compile the Fine Wine 50 Index, were as follows

- **Period between start of 1983 and end of 1986:** 1961, 1962, 1966, 1970, 1975
- **Period between start of 1987 and end of 1989:** 1970, 1975, 1978, 1979, 1982
- **Period between start of 1990 and end of 1992:** 1978, 1979, 1982, 1983, 1985
- **Period between start of 1993 and end of 1995:** 1979, 1982, 1983, 1985, 1986
- **Period between start of 1996 and end of 1997:** 1982, 1983, 1985, 1986, 1989
- **Period between start of 1998 and end of 2003:** 1982, 1985, 1986, 1989, 1990

APPENDIX 3
EXPECTED RETURN RESULTS
FOR UK DATA FROM 1983 TO 2002

Expected Return Results For Fine Wine, Equities & Government Bonds

Observation Period	Fine Wine 50 Index		FTSE 100 Index		UK Govt. Bonds Index	
	per month	per annum	per month	per annum	per month	per annum
5 Years from 1983 to 1987	1.1%	13.1%	1.4%	16.6%	0.1%	1.6%
5 Years from 1984 to 1988	1.0%	11.9%	1.2%	13.9%	0.0%	0.4%
5 Years from 1985 to 1989	0.8%	9.1%	1.3%	15.8%	0.0%	0.3%
5 Years from 1986 to 1990	0.5%	6.2%	0.9%	10.7%	(0.0%)	(0.1%)
5 Years from 1987 to 1991	0.6%	7.0%	0.9%	10.2%	0.0%	0.5%
5 Years from 1988 to 1992	0.5%	6.0%	1.0%	11.5%	0.1%	1.1%
5 Years from 1989 to 1993	0.6%	6.6%	1.2%	14.3%	0.3%	3.9%
5 Years from 1990 to 1994	0.8%	9.1%	0.5%	5.9%	0.1%	1.4%
5 Years from 1991 to 1995	1.1%	13.3%	1.0%	11.8%	0.3%	3.0%
5 Years from 1992 to 1996	1.8%	21.7%	0.9%	10.9%	0.2%	1.9%
5 Years from 1993 to 1997	2.3%	27.1%	1.0%	12.5%	0.1%	1.4%
5 Years from 1994 to 1998	1.6%	18.9%	1.0%	11.8%	0.1%	1.3%
5 Years from 1995 to 1999	1.4%	17.4%	1.4%	17.1%	0.2%	2.7%
5 Years from 1996 to 2000	1.2%	14.1%	1.0%	11.4%	0.1%	1.8%
5 Years from 1997 to 2001	0.7%	8.9%	0.5%	5.9%	0.1%	1.2%
5 Years from 1998 to 2002	0.2%	3.0%	(0.3%)	(4.0%)	0.1%	0.8%
10 Years from 1983 to 1992	0.8%	9.5%	1.2%	14.1%	0.1%	1.3%
10 Years from 1993 to 2002	1.3%	15.0%	0.4%	4.3%	0.1%	1.1%
20 Years from 1983 to 2002	1.0%	12.3%	0.8%	9.2%	0.1%	1.2%

Expected Return Results For Fine Wine, Equities (Income Reinvested) & Government Bonds

Observation Period	Fine Wine 50 Index		FTSE 100 Index (IR)		UK Govt. Bonds Index	
	per month	per annum	per month	per annum	per month	per annum
5 Years from 1993 to 1997	2.3%	27.1%	1.4%	17.2%	0.1%	1.4%
5 Years from 1994 to 1998	1.6%	18.9%	1.3%	15.6%	0.1%	1.3%
5 Years from 1995 to 1999	1.4%	17.4%	1.7%	20.6%	0.2%	2.7%
5 Years from 1996 to 2000	1.2%	14.1%	1.2%	14.4%	0.1%	1.8%
5 Years from 1997 to 2001	0.7%	8.9%	0.7%	8.4%	0.1%	1.2%
5 Years from 1998 to 2002	0.2%	3.0%	(0.1%)	(1.5%)	0.1%	0.8%
10 Years from 1993 to 2002	1.3%	15.0%	0.7%	7.9%	0.1%	1.1%

APPENDIX 4
STANDARD DEVIATION RESULTS
FOR UK DATA FROM 1983 TO 2002

Standard Deviation Results For Fine Wine, Equities & Government Bonds

Observation Period	Fine Wine 50 Index		FTSE 100 Index		UK Govt. Bonds Index	
	per month	per annum	per month	per annum	per month	per annum
5 Years from 1983 to 1987	3.6%	12.5%	5.8%	20.1%	2.3%	8.0%
5 Years from 1984 to 1988	3.8%	13.0%	5.8%	20.1%	2.2%	7.6%
5 Years from 1985 to 1989	3.8%	13.2%	5.9%	20.4%	2.0%	7.0%
5 Years from 1986 to 1990	2.8%	9.6%	6.1%	21.3%	2.3%	7.9%
5 Years from 1987 to 1991	2.8%	9.6%	6.1%	21.0%	1.9%	6.5%
5 Years from 1988 to 1992	3.0%	10.5%	4.8%	16.7%	1.9%	6.5%
5 Years from 1989 to 1993	3.0%	10.5%	4.8%	16.6%	1.9%	6.5%
5 Years from 1990 to 1994	3.1%	10.8%	4.5%	15.7%	2.0%	7.0%
5 Years from 1991 to 1995	3.3%	11.4%	4.0%	13.9%	1.8%	6.2%
5 Years from 1992 to 1996	3.4%	11.8%	3.6%	12.6%	1.8%	6.2%
5 Years from 1993 to 1997	4.7%	16.4%	3.4%	11.8%	1.6%	5.4%
5 Years from 1994 to 1998	5.2%	17.9%	3.8%	13.2%	1.5%	5.4%
5 Years from 1995 to 1999	5.0%	17.5%	3.5%	12.1%	1.4%	4.8%
5 Years from 1996 to 2000	5.5%	19.1%	4.0%	13.7%	1.3%	4.4%
5 Years from 1997 to 2001	5.7%	19.7%	4.4%	15.1%	1.4%	4.7%
5 Years from 1998 to 2002	4.2%	14.7%	4.7%	16.2%	1.4%	4.8%
10 Years from 1983 to 1992	3.3%	11.5%	5.3%	18.4%	2.1%	7.2%
10 Years from 1993 to 2002	4.6%	15.9%	4.1%	14.3%	1.5%	5.1%
20 Years from 1983 to 2002	4.0%	13.9%	4.8%	16.5%	1.8%	6.2%

Standard Deviation Results For Fine Wine, Equities (Income Reinvested) & Government Bonds

Observation Period	Fine Wine 50 Index		FTSE 100 Index (IR)		UK Govt. Bonds Index	
	per month	per annum	per month	per annum	per month	per annum
5 Years from 1993 to 1997	4.7%	16.4%	3.4%	11.8%	1.6%	5.4%
5 Years from 1994 to 1998	5.2%	17.9%	3.8%	13.2%	1.5%	5.4%
5 Years from 1995 to 1999	5.0%	17.5%	3.5%	12.2%	1.4%	4.8%
5 Years from 1996 to 2000	5.5%	19.1%	4.0%	13.8%	1.3%	4.4%
5 Years from 1997 to 2001	5.7%	19.7%	4.3%	15.0%	1.4%	4.7%
5 Years from 1998 to 2002	4.2%	14.7%	4.7%	16.1%	1.4%	4.8%
10 Years from 1993 to 2002	4.6%	15.9%	4.1%	14.3%	1.5%	5.1%

APPENDIX 5
COMPOUND GROWTH RATE RESULTS
FOR UK DATA FROM 1983 TO 2002

Compound Growth Results For Fine Wine, Equities & Government Bonds

Observation Period	Fine Wine 50 Index		FTSE 100 Index		UK Govt. Bonds Index	
	per month	per annum	per month	per annum	per month	per annum
5 Years from 1983 to 1987	1.0%	12.4%	1.2%	13.9%	0.2%	2.1%
5 Years from 1984 to 1988	0.9%	10.5%	0.9%	10.5%	0.0%	0.2%
5 Years from 1985 to 1989	0.7%	8.1%	1.1%	12.8%	0.0%	0.4%
5 Years from 1986 to 1990	0.6%	6.8%	0.7%	8.1%	(0.0%)	(0.2%)
5 Years from 1987 to 1991	0.5%	6.4%	0.5%	6.4%	0.0%	0.0%
5 Years from 1988 to 1992	0.5%	5.4%	0.8%	9.3%	0.1%	0.7%
5 Years from 1989 to 1993	0.5%	6.3%	0.9%	10.2%	0.3%	3.4%
5 Years from 1990 to 1994	0.7%	8.6%	0.5%	5.4%	0.2%	1.8%
5 Years from 1991 to 1995	1.1%	13.5%	0.9%	10.7%	0.2%	2.3%
5 Years from 1992 to 1996	1.7%	21.0%	0.8%	9.5%	0.1%	1.5%
5 Years from 1993 to 1997	2.1%	25.7%	1.0%	11.7%	0.1%	1.2%
5 Years from 1994 to 1998	1.5%	17.5%	0.9%	10.5%	0.1%	1.4%
5 Years from 1995 to 1999	1.3%	15.8%	1.4%	16.9%	0.2%	2.6%
5 Years from 1996 to 2000	1.0%	11.6%	0.8%	10.1%	0.1%	1.7%
5 Years from 1997 to 2001	0.6%	7.0%	0.3%	4.0%	0.1%	1.1%
5 Years from 1998 to 2002	0.3%	4.1%	(0.5%)	(6.5%)	0.0%	0.4%
10 Years from 1983 to 1992	0.7%	8.9%	1.0%	12.0%	0.1%	1.5%
10 Years from 1993 to 2002	1.1%	13.8%	0.3%	3.2%	0.1%	1.0%
20 Years from 1983 to 2002	0.9%	11.4%	0.6%	7.6%	0.1%	1.2%

Compound Growth Results For Fine Wine, Equities (Income Reinvested) & Government Bonds

Observation Period	Fine Wine 50 Index		FTSE 100 Index (IR)		UK Govt. Bonds Index	
	per month	per annum	per month	per annum	per month	per annum
5 Years from 1993 to 1997	2.1%	25.7%	1.4%	16.3%	0.1%	1.2%
5 Years from 1994 to 1998	1.5%	17.5%	1.2%	14.3%	0.1%	1.4%
5 Years from 1995 to 1999	1.3%	15.8%	1.7%	20.4%	0.2%	2.6%
5 Years from 1996 to 2000	1.0%	11.6%	1.1%	13.1%	0.1%	1.7%
5 Years from 1997 to 2001	0.6%	7.0%	0.5%	6.5%	0.1%	1.1%
5 Years from 1998 to 2002	0.3%	4.1%	(0.3%)	(4.0%)	0.0%	0.4%
10 Years from 1993 to 2002	1.1%	13.8%	0.6%	6.7%	0.1%	1.0%

APPENDIX 6
CORRELATION COEFFICIENT RESULTS
FOR UK DATA FROM 1983 TO 2002

Correlation Coefficient Results For Fine Wine, Equities & Government Bonds

Observation Period	Fine Wine 50 Index/ FTSE 100 Index	Fine Wine 50 Index/ UK Govt. Bonds Index	FTSE 100 Index/ UK Govt. Bonds Index
5 Years from 1983 to 1987	0.06	0.08	0.14
5 Years from 1984 to 1988	0.10	0.10	0.17
5 Years from 1985 to 1989	0.10	0.13	0.12
5 Years from 1986 to 1990	0.10	(0.04)	0.25
5 Years from 1987 to 1991	0.08	(0.14)	0.15
5 Years from 1988 to 1992	(0.04)	(0.16)	0.61
5 Years from 1989 to 1993	(0.15)	(0.20)	0.65
5 Years from 1990 to 1994	(0.16)	(0.18)	0.71
5 Years from 1991 to 1995	(0.10)	(0.07)	0.67
5 Years from 1992 to 1996	(0.08)	(0.06)	0.70
5 Years from 1993 to 1997	0.13	0.09	0.63
5 Years from 1994 to 1998	0.05	0.07	0.38
5 Years from 1995 to 1999	0.01	(0.02)	0.20
5 Years from 1996 to 2000	(0.03)	(0.04)	0.15
5 Years from 1997 to 2001	(0.04)	(0.02)	0.08
5 Years from 1998 to 2002	(0.13)	(0.10)	(0.17)
10 Years from 1983 to 1992	0.02	(0.02)	0.33
10 Years from 1993 to 2002	0.02	0.01	0.19
20 Years from 1983 to 2002	0.02	(0.00)	0.28

Correlation Coefficient Results For Fine Wine, Equities (Income Reinvested) & Government Bonds

Observation Period	Fine Wine 50 Index/ FTSE 100 Index (IR)	Fine Wine 50 Index/ UK Govt. Bonds Index	FTSE 100 Index (IR)/ UK Govt. Bonds Index
5 Years from 1993 to 1997	0.12	0.09	0.63
5 Years from 1994 to 1998	0.06	0.07	0.38
5 Years from 1995 to 1999	0.02	(0.02)	0.21
5 Years from 1996 to 2000	(0.03)	(0.04)	0.15
5 Years from 1997 to 2001	(0.06)	(0.02)	0.09
5 Years from 1998 to 2002	(0.15)	(0.10)	(0.16)
10 Years from 1993 to 2002	0.01	0.01	0.19

APPENDIX 7
OPTIMAL RISK-RETURN EFFICIENT PORTFOLIO RESULTS
FOR UK DATA FROM 1983 TO 2002

Optimal Risk-Return Efficient Portfolio Results For Fine Wine, Equities & Government Bonds

Obervation Period	Weights Fine Wine 50 Index	FTSE 100 Index	UK Govt. Bonds Index	Optimal Risk-Return Efficient Portfolio Expected Return per month	per annum	Standard Deviation per month	per annum
5 Years from 1983 to 1987	63%	37%	0%	1.2%	14.4%	3.2%	11.2%
5 Years from 1984 to 1988	35%	65%	0%	1.1%	13.2%	4.1%	14.3%
5 Years from 1985 to 1989	3%	97%	0%	1.3%	15.6%	5.7%	19.9%
5 Years from 1986 to 1990	0%	100%	0%	0.9%	10.7%	6.1%	21.3%
5 Years from 1987 to 1991	0%	100%	0%	0.9%	10.2%	6.1%	21.0%
5 Years from 1988 to 1992	0%	100%	0%	1.0%	11.5%	4.8%	16.7%
5 Years from 1989 to 1993	0%	100%	0%	1.2%	14.3%	4.8%	16.6%
5 Years from 1990 to 1994	100%	0%	0%	0.8%	9.1%	3.1%	10.8%
5 Years from 1991 to 1995	58%	35%	8%	1.0%	12.0%	2.3%	7.9%
5 Years from 1992 to 1996	77%	23%	0%	1.6%	19.2%	2.7%	9.3%
5 Years from 1993 to 1997	70%	30%	0%	1.9%	22.8%	3.6%	12.5%
5 Years from 1994 to 1998	53%	47%	0%	1.3%	15.6%	3.4%	11.6%
5 Years from 1995 to 1999	32%	65%	3%	1.4%	16.8%	2.8%	9.7%
5 Years from 1996 to 2000	38%	58%	4%	1.0%	12.0%	3.0%	10.6%
5 Years from 1997 to 2001	100%	0%	0%	0.7%	8.9%	5.7%	19.7%
5 Years from 1998 to 2002	100%	0%	0%	0.2%	3.0%	4.2%	14.7%
10 Years from 1983 to 1992	0%	100%	0%	1.2%	14.1%	5.3%	18.4%
10 Years from 1993 to 2002	100%	0%	0%	1.3%	15.0%	4.6%	15.9%
20 Years from 1983 to 2002	91%	9%	0%	1.0%	12.0%	3.7%	12.7%

Optimal Risk-Return Efficient Portfolio Results For Fine Wine, Equities (Income Reinvested) & Government Bonds

Observation Period	Weights			Optimal Risk-Return Efficient Portfolio			
	Fine Wine 50 Index	FTSE 100 Index (IR)	UK Govt. Bonds Index	Expected Return		Standard Deviation	
				per month	per annum	per month	per annum
5 Years from 1993 to 1997	56%	44%	0%	1.9%	22.8%	3.2%	11.1%
5 Years from 1994 to 1998	39%	60%	1%	1.4%	16.8%	3.1%	10.9%
5 Years from 1995 to 1999	28%	69%	3%	1.6%	19.2%	2.8%	9.9%
5 Years from 1996 to 2000	31%	60%	9%	1.1%	13.2%	2.9%	10.1%
5 Years from 1997 to 2001	38%	59%	3%	0.7%	8.4%	3.2%	11.3%
5 Years from 1998 to 2002	100%	0%	0%	0.2%	3.0%	4.2%	14.7%
10 Years from 1993 to 2002	91%	9%	0%	1.2%	14.4%	4.2%	14.5%

APPENDIX 8
LIBOR VERSUS OPTIMAL RISK-RETURN EFFICIENT PORTFOLIO RESULTS FOR UK DATA FROM 1983 TO 2002

| Observation Period | LIBOR Risk Free Rate | | Optimal Risk-Return Efficient Portfolio | | | |
| | | | Expected Return | | Standard Deviation | |
	per month	per annum	per month	per annum	per month	per annum
5 Years from 1983 to 1987	0.9%	10.7%	1.2%	14.4%	3.2%	11.2%
5 Years from 1984 to 1988	0.9%	10.7%	1.1%	13.2%	4.1%	14.3%
5 Years from 1985 to 1989	1.0%	11.5%	1.3%	15.6%	5.7%	19.9%
5 Years from 1986 to 1990	**1.0%**	**12.0%**	0.9%	10.7%	6.1%	21.3%
5 Years from 1987 to 1991	**1.0%**	**12.1%**	0.9%	10.2%	6.1%	21.0%
5 Years from 1988 to 1992	**1.0%**	**12.1%**	1.0%	11.5%	4.8%	16.7%
5 Years from 1989 to 1993	0.9%	11.2%	1.2%	14.3%	4.8%	16.6%
5 Years from 1990 to 1994	**0.8%**	**9.5%**	0.8%	9.1%	3.1%	10.8%
5 Years from 1991 to 1995	0.7%	7.9%	1.0%	12.0%	2.3%	7.9%
5 Years from 1992 to 1996	0.6%	6.8%	1.6%	19.2%	2.7%	9.3%
5 Years from 1993 to 1997	0.5%	6.2%	1.9%	22.8%	3.6%	12.5%
5 Years from 1994 to 1998	0.5%	6.5%	1.3%	15.6%	3.4%	11.6%
5 Years from 1995 to 1999	0.5%	6.5%	1.4%	16.8%	2.8%	9.7%
5 Years from 1996 to 2000	0.5%	6.4%	1.0%	12.0%	3.0%	10.6%
5 Years from 1997 to 2001	0.5%	6.1%	0.7%	8.9%	5.7%	19.7%
5 Years from 1998 to 2002	**0.5%**	**5.6%**	0.2%	3.0%	4.2%	14.7%
10 Years from 1983 to 1992	1.0%	11.5%	1.2%	14.1%	5.3%	18.4%
10 Years from 1993 to 2002	0.6%	7.3%	1.3%	15.0%	4.6%	15.9%
20 Years from 1983 to 2002	0.8%	9.4%	1.0%	12.0%	3.7%	12.7%

LIBOR versus Optimal Risk-Return Efficient Portfolio (using FTSE 100 Index (IR))
Figures in bold represent the preferred investment in the risk free rate
as opposed to an investment in either Fine Wine or Equities

Observation Period	LIBOR Risk Free Rate		Optimal Risk-Return Efficient Portfolio Expected Return		Standard Deviation	
	per month	per annum	per month	per annum	per month	per annum
5 Years from 1993 to 1997	0.5%	6.2%	1.9%	22.8%	3.2%	11.1%
5 Years from 1994 to 1998	0.5%	6.5%	1.4%	16.8%	3.1%	10.9%
5 Years from 1995 to 1999	0.5%	6.5%	1.6%	19.2%	2.8%	9.9%
5 Years from 1996 to 2000	0.5%	6.4%	1.1%	13.2%	2.9%	10.1%
5 Years from 1997 to 2001	0.5%	6.1%	0.7%	8.4%	3.2%	11.3%
5 Years from 1998 to 2002	**0.5%**	**5.6%**	0.2%	3.0%	4.2%	14.7%
10 Years from 1993 to 2002	0.6%	7.3%	1.2%	14.4%	4.2%	14.5%

APPENDIX 9
MAXIMUM-RETURN PORTFOLIO RESULTS
FOR UK DATA FROM 1983 TO 2002

Maximum-Return Portfolio Results For Fine Wine, Equities & Government Bonds

Observation Period	Weights			Maximum-Return Portfolio			
	Fine Wine 50	FTSE 100	UK Govt. Bonds	Expected Return		Standard Deviation	
	Index	Index	Index	per month	per annum	per month	per annum
5 Years from 1983 to 1987	0%	100%	0%	1.4%	16.6%	5.8%	20.1%
5 Years from 1984 to 1988	0%	100%	0%	1.2%	13.9%	5.8%	20.1%
5 Years from 1985 to 1989	0%	100%	0%	1.3%	15.8%	5.9%	20.4%
5 Years from 1986 to 1990	0%	100%	0%	0.9%	10.7%	6.1%	21.3%
5 Years from 1987 to 1991	0%	100%	0%	0.9%	10.2%	6.1%	21.0%
5 Years from 1988 to 1992	0%	100%	0%	1.0%	11.5%	4.8%	16.7%
5 Years from 1989 to 1993	0%	100%	0%	1.2%	14.3%	4.8%	16.6%
5 Years from 1990 to 1994	100%	0%	0%	0.8%	9.1%	3.1%	10.8%
5 Years from 1991 to 1995	100%	0%	0%	1.1%	13.3%	3.3%	11.4%
5 Years from 1992 to 1996	100%	0%	0%	1.8%	21.7%	3.4%	11.8%
5 Years from 1993 to 1997	100%	0%	0%	2.3%	27.1%	4.7%	16.4%
5 Years from 1994 to 1998	100%	0%	0%	1.6%	18.9%	5.2%	17.9%
5 Years from 1995 to 1999	100%	0%	0%	1.4%	17.4%	5.0%	17.5%
5 Years from 1996 to 2000	100%	0%	0%	1.2%	14.1%	5.5%	19.1%
5 Years from 1997 to 2001	100%	0%	0%	0.7%	8.9%	5.7%	19.7%
5 Years from 1998 to 2002	100%	0%	0%	0.2%	3.0%	4.2%	14.7%
10 Years from 1983 to 1992	0%	100%	0%	1.2%	14.1%	5.3%	18.4%
10 Years from 1993 to 2002	100%	0%	0%	1.3%	15.0%	4.6%	15.9%
20 Years from 1983 to 2002	100%	0%	0%	1.0%	12.3%	4.0%	13.9%

Maximum-Return Results For Fine Wine, Equities (Income Reinvested) & Government Bonds

Observation Period	Weights			Maximum-Return Portfolio			
	Fine Wine 50 Index	FTSE 100 Index (IR)	UK Govt. Bonds Index	Expected Return		Standard Deviation	
				per month	per annum	per month	per annum
5 Years from 1993 to 1997	100%	0%	0%	2.3%	27.1%	4.7%	16.4%
5 Years from 1994 to 1998	100%	0%	0%	1.6%	18.9%	5.2%	17.9%
5 Years from 1995 to 1999	0%	100%	0%	1.7%	20.6%	3.5%	12.2%
5 Years from 1996 to 2000	0%	100%	0%	1.2%	14.4%	4.0%	13.8%
5 Years from 1997 to 2001	100%	0%	0%	0.7%	8.9%	5.7%	19.7%
5 Years from 1998 to 2002	100%	0%	0%	0.2%	3.0%	4.2%	14.7%
10 Years from 1993 to 2002	100%	0%	0%	1.3%	15.0%	4.6%	15.9%

APPENDIX 10
MINIMUM-RISK PORTFOLIO RESULTS
FOR UK DATA FROM 1983 TO 2002

	Fine Wine 50 Index	FTSE 100 Index	UK Govt. Bonds Index	Expected Return		Standard Deviation	
				per month	per annum	per month	per annum
5 Years from 1983 to 1987	28%	8%	64%	0.5%	6.0%	2.0%	6.8%
5 Years from 1984 to 1988	22%	5%	73%	0.3%	3.6%	1.9%	6.7%
5 Years from 1985 to 1989	16%	4%	80%	0.2%	2.4%	1.8%	6.4%
5 Years from 1986 to 1990	40%	0%	60%	0.2%	2.4%	1.7%	6.0%
5 Years from 1987 to 1991	29%	0%	71%	0.2%	2.4%	1.5%	5.1%
5 Years from 1988 to 1992	26%	0%	74%	0.2%	2.4%	1.5%	5.1%
5 Years from 1989 to 1993	33%	0%	67%	0.4%	4.8%	1.4%	5.0%
5 Years from 1990 to 1994	28%	0%	72%	0.3%	3.6%	1.6%	5.4%
5 Years from 1991 to 1995	29%	0%	71%	0.5%	6.0%	1.5%	5.3%
5 Years from 1992 to 1996	21%	0%	79%	0.5%	6.0%	1.6%	5.4%
5 Years from 1993 to 1997	9%	0%	91%	0.3%	3.6%	1.5%	5.3%
5 Years from 1994 to 1998	6%	0%	94%	0.2%	2.4%	1.5%	5.2%
5 Years from 1995 to 1999	7%	7%	86%	0.4%	4.8%	1.3%	4.5%
5 Years from 1996 to 2000	8%	9%	83%	0.3%	3.6%	1.2%	4.2%
5 Years from 1997 to 2001	9%	10%	81%	0.2%	2.4%	1.3%	4.5%
5 Years from 1998 to 2002	6%	20%	74%	0.0%	0.0%	1.2%	4.3%
10 Years from 1983 to 1992	27%	0%	73%	0.3%	3.6%	1.8%	6.1%
10 Years from 1993 to 2002	8%	5%	87%	0.2%	2.4%	1.4%	4.8%
20 Years from 1983 to 2002	18%	4%	78%	0.3%	3.6%	1.6%	5.7%

Minimum-Risk Results For Fine Wine, Equities (Income Reinvested) & Government Bonds

Observation Period	Weights			Minimum-Risk Portfolio			
	Fine Wine 50	FTSE 100	UK Govt. Bonds	Expected Return		Standard Deviation	
	Index	Index (IR)	Index	per month	per annum	per month	per annum
5 Years from 1993 to 1997	9%	0%	91%	0.3%	3.6%	1.5%	5.3%
5 Years from 1994 to 1998	6%	0%	94%	0.2%	2.4%	1.5%	5.2%
5 Years from 1995 to 1999	7%	6%	87%	0.4%	4.8%	1.3%	4.5%
5 Years from 1996 to 2000	7%	8%	85%	0.3%	3.6%	1.2%	4.2%
5 Years from 1997 to 2001	7%	9%	84%	0.2%	2.4%	1.3%	4.5%
5 Years from 1998 to 2002	21%	3%	76%	0.1%	1.2%	1.3%	4.5%
10 Years from 1993 to 2002	7%	4%	89%	0.2%	2.4%	1.4%	4.8%

APPENDIX 11
OPTIMAL RISK-RETURN EFFICIENT PORTFOLIO RESULTS FOR UK DATA FROM 1983 TO 2002

	Index	Index	per month	per annum	per month	per annum
5 Years from 1983 to 1987	100%	0%	1.4%	16.6%	5.8%	20.1%
5 Years from 1984 to 1988	100%	0%	1.2%	13.9%	5.8%	20.1%
5 Years from 1985 to 1989	100%	0%	1.3%	15.8%	5.9%	20.4%
5 Years from 1986 to 1990	100%	0%	0.9%	10.7%	6.1%	21.3%
5 Years from 1987 to 1991	100%	0%	0.9%	10.2%	6.1%	21.0%
5 Years from 1988 to 1992	100%	0%	1.0%	11.5%	4.8%	16.7%
5 Years from 1989 to 1993	100%	0%	1.2%	14.3%	4.8%	16.6%
5 Years from 1990 to 1994	100%	0%	0.5%	5.9%	4.5%	15.7%
5 Years from 1991 to 1995	100%	0%	1.0%	11.8%	4.0%	13.9%
5 Years from 1992 to 1996	100%	0%	0.9%	10.9%	3.6%	12.6%
5 Years from 1993 to 1997	100%	0%	1.0%	12.5%	3.4%	11.8%
5 Years from 1994 to 1998	100%	0%	1.0%	11.8%	3.8%	13.2%
5 Years from 1995 to 1999	100%	0%	1.4%	17.1%	3.5%	12.1%
5 Years from 1996 to 2000	100%	0%	1.0%	11.4%	4.0%	13.7%
5 Years from 1997 to 2001	100%	0%	0.5%	5.9%	4.4%	15.1%
5 Years from 1998 to 2002	0%	100%	0.1%	0.8%	1.4%	4.8%
10 Years from 1983 to 1992	100%	0%	1.2%	14.1%	5.3%	18.4%
10 Years from 1993 to 2002	100%	0%	0.4%	4.3%	4.1%	14.3%
20 Years from 1983 to 2002	100%	0%	0.8%	9.2%	4.8%	16.5%

Optimal Risk-Return Portfolio Results For Equities (Income Reinvested) & Government Bonds Only

Observation Period	Weights		Optimal Risk-Return Efficient Portfolio			
	FTSE 100 Index (IR)	UK Govt. Bonds Index	Expected Return		Standard Deviation	
			per month	per annum	per month	per annum
5 Years from 1993 to 1997	100%	0%	1.4%	17.2%	3.4%	11.8%
5 Years from 1994 to 1998	100%	0%	1.3%	15.6%	3.8%	13.2%
5 Years from 1995 to 1999	99%	1%	1.7%	20.4%	3.5%	12.1%
5 Years from 1996 to 2000	100%	0%	1.2%	14.4%	4.0%	13.8%
5 Years from 1997 to 2001	100%	0%	0.7%	8.4%	4.3%	15.0%
5 Years from 1998 to 2002	0%	100%	0.1%	0.8%	1.4%	4.8%
10 Years from 1993 to 2002	100%	0%	0.7%	7.9%	4.1%	14.3%

APPENDIX 12
MAXIMUM-RETURN PORTFOLIO RESULTS—EQUITIES & BONDS ONLY FOR UK DATA FROM 1983 TO 2002

Maximum-Return Portfolio Results For Equities & Government Bonds Only

Observation Period	Weights		Maximum-Return Portfolio			
	FTSE 100 Index	UK Govt. Bonds Index	Expected Return		Standard Deviation	
			per month	per annum	per month	per annum
5 Years from 1983 to 1987	100%	0%	1.4%	16.6%	5.8%	20.1%
5 Years from 1984 to 1988	100%	0%	1.2%	13.9%	5.8%	20.1%
5 Years from 1985 to 1989	100%	0%	1.3%	15.8%	5.9%	20.4%
5 Years from 1986 to 1990	100%	0%	0.9%	10.7%	6.1%	21.3%
5 Years from 1987 to 1991	100%	0%	0.9%	10.2%	6.1%	21.0%
5 Years from 1988 to 1992	100%	0%	1.0%	11.5%	4.8%	16.7%
5 Years from 1989 to 1993	100%	0%	1.2%	14.3%	4.8%	16.6%
5 Years from 1990 to 1994	100%	0%	0.5%	5.9%	4.5%	15.7%
5 Years from 1991 to 1995	100%	0%	1.0%	11.8%	4.0%	13.9%
5 Years from 1992 to 1996	100%	0%	0.9%	10.9%	3.6%	12.6%
5 Years from 1993 to 1997	100%	0%	1.0%	12.5%	3.4%	11.8%
5 Years from 1994 to 1998	100%	0%	1.0%	11.8%	3.8%	13.2%
5 Years from 1995 to 1999	100%	0%	1.4%	17.1%	3.5%	12.1%
5 Years from 1996 to 2000	100%	0%	1.0%	11.4%	4.0%	13.7%
5 Years from 1997 to 2001	100%	0%	0.5%	5.9%	4.4%	15.1%
5 Years from 1998 to 2002	0%	100%	0.1%	0.8%	1.4%	4.8%
10 Years from 1983 to 1992	100%	0%	1.2%	14.1%	5.3%	18.4%
10 Years from 1993 to 2002	100%	0%	0.4%	4.3%	4.1%	14.3%
20 Years from 1983 to 2002	100%	0%	0.8%	9.2%	4.8%	16.5%

Maximum-Return Portfolio Results For Equities (Income Reinvested) & Government Bonds Only

Observation Period	Weights		Maximum-Return Portfolio			
	FTSE 100	UK Govt. Bonds	Expected Return		Standard Deviation	
	Index (IR)	Index	per month	per annum	per month	per annum
5 Years from 1993 to 1997	100%	0%	1.4%	17.2%	3.4%	11.8%
5 Years from 1994 to 1998	100%	0%	1.3%	15.6%	3.8%	13.2%
5 Years from 1995 to 1999	100%	0%	1.7%	20.6%	3.5%	12.2%
5 Years from 1996 to 2000	100%	0%	1.2%	14.4%	4.0%	13.8%
5 Years from 1997 to 2001	100%	0%	0.7%	8.4%	4.3%	15.0%
5 Years from 1998 to 2002	0%	100%	0.1%	0.8%	1.4%	4.8%
10 Years from 1993 to 2002	100%	0%	0.7%	7.9%	4.1%	14.3%

APPENDIX 13
MINIMUM-RISK PORTFOLIO RESULTS—EQUITIES & BONDS ONLY FOR UK DATA FROM 1983 TO 2002

Minimum-Risk Portfolio Results For Equities & Government Bonds Only

Observation Period	Weights		Minimum-Risk Portfolio			
	FTSE 100 Index	UK Govt. Bonds Index	Expected Return		Standard Deviation	
			per month	per annum	per month	per annum
5 Years from 1983 to 1987	14%	86%	0.3%	3.6%	2.2%	7.8%
5 Years from 1984 to 1988	6%	94%	0.1%	1.2%	2.1%	7.4%
5 Years from 1985 to 1989	6%	94%	0.1%	1.2%	2.0%	6.8%
5 Years from 1986 to 1990	1%	99%	0.0%	0.0%	2.3%	7.9%
5 Years from 1987 to 1991	7%	93%	0.1%	1.2%	1.9%	6.4%
5 Years from 1988 to 1992	0%	100%	0.1%	1.1%	1.9%	6.5%
5 Years from 1989 to 1993	0%	100%	0.3%	3.9%	1.9%	6.5%
5 Years from 1990 to 1994	0%	100%	0.1%	1.4%	2.0%	7.0%
5 Years from 1991 to 1995	0%	100%	0.3%	3.0%	1.8%	6.2%
5 Years from 1992 to 1996	0%	100%	0.2%	1.9%	1.8%	6.2%
5 Years from 1993 to 1997	0%	100%	0.1%	1.4%	1.6%	5.4%
5 Years from 1994 to 1998	0%	100%	0.1%	1.3%	1.5%	5.4%
5 Years from 1995 to 1999	6%	94%	0.3%	3.6%	1.4%	4.7%
5 Years from 1996 to 2000	6%	94%	0.2%	2.4%	1.2%	4.3%
5 Years from 1997 to 2001	0%	100%	0.1%	1.2%	1.4%	4.7%
5 Years from 1998 to 2002	17%	83%	0.0%	0.0%	1.3%	4.4%
10 Years from 1983 to 1992	0%	100%	0.1%	1.3%	2.1%	7.2%
10 Years from 1993 to 2002	3%	97%	0.1%	1.2%	1.5%	5.0%
20 Years from 1983 to 2002	0%	100%	0.1%	1.2%	1.8%	6.2%

Minimum-Risk Portfolio Results For Equities (Income Reinvested) & Government Bonds Only

Observation Period	Weights		Minimum-Risk Portfolio			
	FTSE 100	UK Govt. Bonds	Expected Return		Standard Deviation	
	Index (IR)	Index	per month	per annum	per month	per annum
5 Years from 1993 to 1997	0%	100%	0.1%	1.4%	1.6%	5.4%
5 Years from 1994 to 1998	0%	100%	0.1%	1.3%	1.5%	5.4%
5 Years from 1995 to 1999	5%	95%	0.3%	3.6%	1.4%	4.7%
5 Years from 1996 to 2000	5%	95%	0.1%	1.8%	1.3%	4.4%
5 Years from 1997 to 2001	0%	100%	0.1%	1.2%	1.4%	4.7%
5 Years from 1998 to 2002	0%	100%	0.1%	0.8%	1.4%	4.8%
10 Years from 1993 to 2002	1%	99%	0.1%	1.2%	1.5%	5.1%

APPENDIX 14
SHARPE RATIO RESULTS
FOR UK DATA FROM 1983 TO 2002

Sharpe Ratio Results For Fine Wine, Equities & Government Bonds

Observation Period	3 Asset Portfolio Fine Wine 50 Index/ FTSE 100 Index/ UK Govt. Bonds Index	2 Asset Portfolio FTSE 100 Index/ UK Govt. Bonds Index
5 Years from 1983 to 1987	0.10	0.09
5 Years from 1984 to 1988	0.05	0.05
5 Years from 1985 to 1989	0.06	0.06
5 Years from 1986 to 1990	(0.02)	(0.02)
5 Years from 1987 to 1991	(0.03)	(0.03)
5 Years from 1988 to 1992	(0.01)	(0.01)
5 Years from 1989 to 1993	0.05	0.05
5 Years from 1990 to 1994	(0.01)	(0.07)
5 Years from 1991 to 1995	0.15	0.08
5 Years from 1992 to 1996	0.38	0.09
5 Years from 1993 to 1997	0.38	0.15
5 Years from 1994 to 1998	0.23	0.12
5 Years from 1995 to 1999	0.31	0.25
5 Years from 1996 to 2000	0.15	0.11
5 Years from 1997 to 2001	0.04	(0.00)
5 Years from 1998 to 2002	(0.05)	(0.29)
10 Years from 1983 to 1992	0.04	0.04
10 Years from 1993 to 2002	0.14	(0.06)
20 Years from 1983 to 2002	0.06	(0.00)

Sharpe Ratio Results For Fine Wine, Equities (Income Reinvested) & Govt. Bonds

Observation Period	3 Asset Portfolio Fine Wine 50 Index/ FTSE 100 Index (IR)/ UK Govt. Bonds Index	2 Asset Portfolio FTSE 100 Index (IR)/ UK Govt. Bonds Index
5 Years from 1993 to 1997	0.43	0.27
5 Years from 1994 to 1998	0.27	0.20
5 Years from 1995 to 1999	0.37	0.33
5 Years from 1996 to 2000	0.20	0.17
5 Years from 1997 to 2001	0.06	0.04
5 Years from 1998 to 2002	(0.05)	(0.29)
10 Years from 1993 to 2002	0.14	0.01

APPENDIX 15
BETA RESULTS
FOR UK DATA FROM 1983 TO 2002

Beta Value Results For Fine Wine & Equities Only

Observation Period	Beta Value
5 Years from 1983 to 1987	0.04
5 Years from 1984 to 1988	0.06
5 Years from 1985 to 1989	0.06
5 Years from 1986 to 1990	0.04
5 Years from 1987 to 1991	0.04
5 Years from 1988 to 1992	(0.03)
5 Years from 1989 to 1993	(0.10)
5 Years from 1990 to 1994	(0.11)
5 Years from 1991 to 1995	(0.08)
5 Years from 1992 to 1996	(0.07)
5 Years from 1993 to 1997	0.17
5 Years from 1994 to 1998	0.07
5 Years from 1995 to 1999	0.02
5 Years from 1996 to 2000	(0.05)
5 Years from 1997 to 2001	(0.06)
5 Years from 1998 to 2002	(0.11)
10 Years from 1983 to 1992	0.01
10 Years from 1993 to 2002	0.03
20 Years from 1983 to 2002	0.01

Beta Value Results For Fine Wine & Equities (Income Reinvested) Only

Observation Period	Beta Value
5 Years from 1993 to 1997	0.16
5 Years from 1994 to 1998	0.07
5 Years from 1995 to 1999	0.03
5 Years from 1996 to 2000	(0.04)
5 Years from 1997 to 2001	(0.08)
5 Years from 1998 to 2002	(0.14)
10 Years from 1993 to 2002	0.01

APPENDIX 16
CAPM RESULTS
FOR UK DATA FROM 1983 TO 2002

CAPM Results For Fine Wine & Equities Only

Observation Period	CAPM Expected Return		Fine Wine 50 Index Expected Return		% Change
	per month	per annum	per month	per annum	
5 Years from 1983 to 1987	0.9%	10.9%	1.1%	13.1%	19.8%
5 Years from 1984 to 1988	0.9%	10.9%	1.0%	11.9%	9.8%
5 Years from 1985 to 1989	1.0%	11.8%	0.8%	9.1%	(22.8%)
5 Years from 1986 to 1990	1.0%	11.9%	0.5%	6.2%	(48.3%)
5 Years from 1987 to 1991	1.0%	12.0%	0.6%	7.0%	(42.0%)
5 Years from 1988 to 1992	1.0%	12.1%	0.5%	6.0%	(50.6%)
5 Years from 1989 to 1993	0.9%	10.9%	0.6%	6.6%	(39.1%)
5 Years from 1990 to 1994	0.8%	9.9%	0.8%	9.1%	(8.0%)
5 Years from 1991 to 1995	0.6%	7.6%	1.1%	13.3%	74.7%
5 Years from 1992 to 1996	0.5%	6.6%	1.8%	21.7%	231.4%
5 Years from 1993 to 1997	0.6%	7.3%	2.3%	27.1%	269.5%
5 Years from 1994 to 1998	0.6%	6.8%	1.6%	18.9%	177.0%
5 Years from 1995 to 1999	0.6%	6.6%	1.4%	17.4%	161.5%
5 Years from 1996 to 2000	0.5%	6.1%	1.2%	14.1%	129.9%
5 Years from 1997 to 2001	0.5%	6.1%	0.7%	8.9%	45.7%
5 Years from 1998 to 2002	0.6%	6.7%	0.2%	3.0%	(55.5%)
10 Years from 1983 to 1992	1.0%	11.6%	0.8%	9.5%	(17.5%)
10 Years from 1993 to 2002	0.6%	7.2%	1.3%	15.0%	107.8%
20 Years from 1983 to 2002	0.8%	9.4%	1.0%	12.3%	31.3%

CAPM Results For Fine Wine & Equities (Income Reinvested) Only

Observation Period	CAPM Expected Return		Fine Wine 50 Index (IR) Expected Return		% Change
	per month	per annum	per month	per annum	
5 Years from 1993 to 1997	0.7%	8.0%	2.3%	27.1%	239.5%
5 Years from 1994 to 1998	0.6%	7.2%	1.6%	18.9%	164.7%
5 Years from 1995 to 1999	0.6%	6.8%	1.4%	17.4%	154.1%
5 Years from 1996 to 2000	0.5%	6.0%	1.2%	14.1%	134.3%
5 Years from 1997 to 2001	0.5%	5.9%	0.7%	8.9%	50.6%
5 Years from 1998 to 2002	0.6%	6.6%	0.2%	3.0%	(54.7%)
10 Years from 1993 to 2002	0.6%	7.3%	1.3%	15.0%	105.4%

APPENDIX 17
CAPM ANALYSIS
FOR UK DATA FROM 1983 TO 2002

CAPM Analysis For Fine Wine & Equities Only
where it indicates to not invest in the Fine Wine 50 Index, an investment in equities or in the risk free asset is preferred

Observation Period	CAPM Analysis
5 Years from 1983 to 1987	INVEST in FW50 Index: RETURN c.20% > CONTRIBUTION to OVERALL PORTFOLIO RISK
5 Years from 1984 to 1988	INVEST in FW50 Index: RETURN c.10% > CONTRIBUTION to OVERALL PORTFOLIO RISK
5 Years from 1985 to 1989	DO NOT INVEST in FW50 Index: RETURN c.23% < CONTRIBUTION to OVERALL PORTFOLIO RISK
5 Years from 1986 to 1990	DO NOT INVEST in FW50 Index: RETURN c.48% < CONTRIBUTION to OVERALL PORTFOLIO RISK
5 Years from 1987 to 1991	DO NOT INVEST in FW50 Index: RETURN c.42% < CONTRIBUTION to OVERALL PORTFOLIO RISK
5 Years from 1988 to 1992	DO NOT INVEST in FW50 Index: RETURN c.51% < CONTRIBUTION to OVERALL PORTFOLIO RISK
5 Years from 1989 to 1993	DO NOT INVEST in FW50 Index: RETURN c.39% < CONTRIBUTION to OVERALL PORTFOLIO RISK
5 Years from 1990 to 1994	DO NOT INVEST in FW50 Index: RETURN c.8% < CONTRIBUTION to OVERALL PORTFOLIO RISK
5 Years from 1991 to 1995	INVEST in FW50 Index: RETURN c.75% > CONTRIBUTION to OVERALL PORTFOLIO RISK
5 Years from 1992 to 1996	INVEST in FW50 Index: RETURN c.231% > CONTRIBUTION to OVERALL PORTFOLIO RISK
5 Years from 1993 to 1997	INVEST in FW50 Index: RETURN c.269% > CONTRIBUTION to OVERALL PORTFOLIO RISK
5 Years from 1994 to 1998	INVEST in FW50 Index: RETURN c.177% > CONTRIBUTION to OVERALL PORTFOLIO RISK
5 Years from 1995 to 1999	INVEST in FW50 Index: RETURN c.162% > CONTRIBUTION to OVERALL PORTFOLIO RISK
5 Years from 1996 to 2000	INVEST in FW50 Index: RETURN c.130% > CONTRIBUTION to OVERALL PORTFOLIO RISK
5 Years from 1997 to 2001	INVEST in FW50 Index: RETURN c.46% > CONTRIBUTION to OVERALL PORTFOLIO RISK
5 Years from 1998 to 2002	DO NOT INVEST in FW50 Index: RETURN c.56% < CONTRIBUTION to OVERALL PORTFOLIO RISK
10 Years from 1983 to 1992	DO NOT INVEST in FW50 Index: RETURN c.18% < CONTRIBUTION to OVERALL PORTFOLIO RISK
10 Years from 1993 to 2002	INVEST in FW50 Index: RETURN c.108% > CONTRIBUTION to OVERALL PORTFOLIO RISK
20 Years from 1983 to 2002	INVEST in FW50 Index: RETURN c.31% > CONTRIBUTION to OVERALL PORTFOLIO RISK

CAPM Analysis For Fine Wine & Equities (Income Reinvested) Only

Observation Period	CAPM Analysis
5 Years from 1993 to 1997	INVEST in FW50 Index: RETURN c.240% > CONTRIBUTION to OVERALL PORTFOLIO RISK
5 Years from 1994 to 1998	INVEST in FW50 Index: RETURN c.165% > CONTRIBUTION to OVERALL PORTFOLIO RISK
5 Years from 1995 to 1999	INVEST in FW50 Index: RETURN c.154% > CONTRIBUTION to OVERALL PORTFOLIO RISK
5 Years from 1996 to 2000	INVEST in FW50 Index: RETURN c.134% > CONTRIBUTION to OVERALL PORTFOLIO RISK
5 Years from 1997 to 2001	INVEST in FW50 Index: RETURN c.51% > CONTRIBUTION to OVERALL PORTFOLIO RISK
5 Years from 1998 to 2002	DO NOT INVEST in FW50 Index: RETURN c.55% < CONTRIBUTION to OVERALL PORTFOLIO RISK

APPENDIX 18
EXPECTED RETURN RESULTS FOR UK & US DATA
INCORPORATING 2003 DATA FROM 1983 TO 2003

Expected Return Results For Fine Wine, Equities & Government Bonds

	UK Data					
Observation Period	Fine Wine 50 Index		FTSE 100 Index		UK Govt. Bonds Index	
	per month	per annum	per month	per annum	per month	per annum
5 Years from 1998 to 2002	0.2%	3.0%	(0.3%)	(4.0%)	0.1%	0.8%
5 Years from 1999 to 2003	0.7%	8.6%	(0.4%)	(4.2%)	(0.2%)	(1.9%)
10 Years from 1983 to 1992	0.8%	9.5%	1.2%	14.1%	0.1%	1.3%
10 Years from 1993 to 2002	1.3%	15.0%	0.4%	4.3%	0.1%	1.1%
10 Years from 1994 to 2003	1.1%	13.8%	0.3%	3.8%	(0.0%)	(0.3%)
11 Years from 1993 to 2003	1.2%	13.9%	0.4%	5.2%	0.1%	0.7%
20 Years from 1983 to 2002	1.0%	12.3%	0.8%	9.2%	0.1%	1.2%
20 Years from 1984 to 2003	1.0%	11.5%	0.7%	8.9%	0.1%	0.9%
21 Years from 1983 to 2003	1.0%	11.8%	0.8%	9.4%	0.1%	1.0%

	US Data					
Observation Period	Fine Wine 50 Index		Dow Jones Index		US 30 Yr Treas. Bonds Index	
	per month	per annum	per month	per annum	per month	per annum
5 Years from 1998 to 2002	0.2%	3.0%	0.2%	2.9%	(0.0%)	(0.3%)
5 Years from 1999 to 2003	0.7%	8.6%	0.3%	4.1%	0.0%	0.1%
10 Years from 1983 to 1992	0.8%	9.5%	1.1%	12.8%	(0.0%)	(0.2%)
10 Years from 1993 to 2002	1.3%	15.0%	0.9%	10.6%	(0.0%)	(0.3%)
10 Years from 1994 to 2003	1.1%	13.8%	1.0%	11.6%	(0.0%)	(0.1%)
11 Years from 1993 to 2003	1.2%	13.9%	1.0%	11.7%	(0.0%)	(0.2%)
20 Years from 1983 to 2002	1.0%	12.3%	1.0%	11.7%	(0.0%)	(0.3%)
20 Years from 1984 to 2003	1.0%	11.5%	1.0%	11.9%	(0.0%)	(0.3%)
21 Years from 1983 to 2003	1.0%	11.8%	1.0%	12.3%	(0.0%)	(0.2%)

APPENDIX 19
STANDARD DEVIATION RESULTS FOR UK & US DATA INCORPORATING 2003 DATA FROM 1983 TO 2003

Standard Deviation Results For Fine Wine, Equities & Government Bonds

Observation Period	UK Data					
	Fine Wine 50 Index		FTSE 100 Index		UK Govt. Bonds Index	
	per month	per annum	per month	per annum	per month	per annum
5 Years from 1998 to 2002	4.2%	14.7%	4.7%	16.2%	1.4%	4.8%
5 Years from 1999 to 2003	3.9%	13.4%	4.6%	15.8%	1.3%	4.5%
10 Years from 1983 to 1992	3.3%	11.5%	5.3%	18.4%	2.1%	7.2%
10 Years from 1993 to 2002	4.6%	15.9%	4.1%	14.3%	1.5%	5.1%
10 Years from 1994 to 2003	4.6%	15.8%	4.2%	14.7%	1.4%	4.9%
11 Years from 1993 to 2003	4.4%	15.4%	4.1%	14.4%	1.4%	5.0%
20 Years from 1983 to 2002	4.0%	13.9%	4.8%	16.5%	1.8%	6.2%
20 Years from 1984 to 2003	4.0%	13.9%	4.8%	16.7%	1.8%	6.1%
21 Years from 1983 to 2003	3.9%	13.7%	4.7%	16.4%	1.8%	6.1%

Observation Period	US Data					
	Fine Wine 50 Index		Dow Jones Index		US 30 Yr Treas. Bonds Index	
	per month	per annum	per month	per annum	per month	per annum
5 Years from 1998 to 2002	4.2%	14.7%	5.5%	19.1%	0.3%	1.1%
5 Years from 1999 to 2003	3.9%	13.4%	5.1%	17.5%	0.4%	1.3%
10 Years from 1983 to 1992	3.3%	11.5%	4.6%	16.0%	0.3%	1.1%
10 Years from 1993 to 2002	4.6%	15.9%	4.6%	16.0%	0.3%	1.1%
10 Years from 1994 to 2003	4.6%	15.8%	4.7%	16.3%	0.3%	1.2%
11 Years from 1993 to 2003	4.4%	15.4%	4.5%	15.6%	0.3%	1.2%
20 Years from 1983 to 2002	4.0%	13.9%	4.6%	15.9%	0.3%	1.1%
20 Years from 1984 to 2003	4.0%	13.9%	4.6%	16.0%	0.3%	1.1%
21 Years from 1983 to 2003	3.9%	13.7%	4.5%	15.8%	0.3%	1.1%

APPENDIX 20
COMPOUND GROWTH RATE RESULTS FOR UK & US DATA
INCORPORATING 2003 DATA FROM 1983 TO 2003

Compound Growth Results For Fine Wine, Equities & Government Bonds

| Observation Period | UK Data | | | | | |
| | Fine Wine 50 Index | | FTSE 100 Index | | UK Govt. Bonds Index | |
	per month	per annum	per month	per annum	per month	per annum
5 Years from 1998 to 2002	0.3%	4.1%	(0.5%)	(6.5%)	0.0%	0.4%
5 Years from 1999 to 2003	0.7%	7.9%	(0.5%)	(5.5%)	(0.2%)	(2.3%)
10 Years from 1983 to 199:	0.7%	8.9%	1.0%	12.0%	0.1%	1.5%
10 Years from 1993 to 200:	1.1%	13.8%	0.3%	3.2%	0.1%	1.0%
10 Years from 1994 to 200:	1.1%	12.7%	0.2%	2.5%	(0.0%)	(0.4%)
11 Years from 1993 to 200:	1.1%	12.7%	0.3%	4.1%	0.1%	0.6%
20 Years from 1983 to 200:	0.9%	11.4%	0.6%	7.6%	0.1%	1.2%
20 Years from 1984 to 200:	0.9%	10.4%	0.6%	7.2%	0.1%	0.7%
21 Years from 1983 to 200:	0.9%	10.9%	0.7%	7.9%	0.1%	1.0%

| Observation Period | US Data | | | | | |
| | Fine Wine 50 Index | | Dow Jones Index | | US 30 Yr Treas. Bonds Inde: | |
	per month	per annum	per month	per annum	per month	per annum
5 Years from 1998 to 2002	0.3%	4.1%	0.1%	1.1%	(0.3%)	(3.8%)
5 Years from 1999 to 2003	0.7%	7.9%	0.2%	2.2%	(0.0%)	(0.1%)
10 Years from 1983 to 199:	0.7%	8.9%	0.9%	11.3%	(0.3%)	(4.0%)
10 Years from 1993 to 200:	1.1%	13.8%	0.8%	9.2%	(0.3%)	(4.1%)
10 Years from 1994 to 200:	1.1%	12.7%	0.8%	9.7%	(0.2%)	(2.0%)
11 Years from 1993 to 200:	1.1%	12.7%	0.9%	10.6%	(0.3%)	(3.2%)
20 Years from 1983 to 200:	0.9%	11.4%	0.9%	10.3%	(0.4%)	(4.2%)
20 Years from 1984 to 200:	0.9%	10.4%	0.9%	10.8%	(0.4%)	(4.2%)
21 Years from 1983 to 200:	0.9%	10.9%	0.9%	10.9%	(0.3%)	(3.8%)

APPENDIX 21
CORRELATION COEFFICIENT RESULTS FOR UK & US DATA INCORPORATING 2003 DATA FROM 1983 TO 2003

Correlation Coefficient Results For Fine Wine, Equities & Government Bonds

Observation Period	UK Data		
	Fine Wine 50 Index FTSE 100 Index	Fine Wine 50 Index/ Govt. Bonds Index	FTSE 100 Index/ Govt. Bonds Index
5 Years from 1998 to 2002	(0.13)	(0.10)	(0.17)
5 Years from 1999 to 2003	0.02	(0.04)	(0.23)
10 Years from 1983 to 1992	0.02	(0.02)	0.33
10 Years from 1993 to 2002	0.02	0.01	0.19
10 Years from 1994 to 2003	0.05	0.04	0.09
11 Years from 1993 to 2003	0.03	0.02	0.14
20 Years from 1983 to 2002	0.02	(0.00)	0.28
20 Years from 1984 to 2003	0.02	0.00	0.27
21 Years from 1983 to 2003	0.02	(0.00)	0.26

Observation Period	US Data		
	Fine Wine 50 Index Dow Jones Index	Fine Wine 50 Index/ US 30 Yr Treas. Bonds Index	Dow Jones Index / US 30 Yr Treas. Bonds Index
5 Years from 1998 to 2002	(0.05)	0.11	0.37
5 Years from 1999 to 2003	0.06	0.06	0.29
10 Years from 1983 to 1992	0.05	0.06	(0.29)
10 Years from 1993 to 2002	0.01	0.04	0.08
10 Years from 1994 to 2003	0.03	(0.02)	0.10
11 Years from 1993 to 2003	0.02	0.01	0.09
20 Years from 1983 to 2002	0.03	0.05	(0.11)
20 Years from 1984 to 2003	0.03	0.03	(0.07)
21 Years from 1983 to 2003	0.03	0.03	(0.09)

APPENDIX 22
OPTIMAL RISK-RETURN EFFICIENT PORTFOLIO RESULTS FOR UK & US DATA INCORPORATING 2003 DATA FROM 1983 TO 2003

Optimal Risk-Return Efficient Portfolio Results For Fine Wine, Equities & Government Bonds

UK Data

| Observation Period | Weights | | | Optimal Risk-Return Efficient Portfolio | | | |
| | Fine Wine 50 Index | FTSE 100 Index | UK Govt. Bonds Index | Expected Return | | Standard Deviation | |
				per month	per annum	per month	per annum
5 Years from 1998 to 2002	100%	0%	0%	0.2%	3.0%	4.2%	14.7%
5 Years from 1999 to 2003	98%	0%	2%	0.7%	8.4%	3.8%	13.1%
10 Years from 1983 to 1992	0%	100%	0%	1.2%	14.1%	5.3%	18.4%
10 Years from 1993 to 2002	100%	0%	0%	1.3%	15.0%	4.6%	15.9%
10 Years from 1994 to 2003	100%	0%	0%	1.1%	13.8%	4.6%	15.8%
11 Years from 1993 to 2003	92%	8%	0%	1.1%	13.2%	4.1%	14.2%
20 Years from 1983 to 2002	91%	9%	0%	1.0%	12.0%	3.7%	12.7%
20 Years from 1984 to 2003	72%	28%	0%	0.9%	10.8%	3.2%	11.1%
21 Years from 1983 to 2003	100%	0%	0%	1.0%	11.8%	3.9%	13.7%

US Data

| Observation Period | Weights | | | Optimal Risk-Return Efficient Portfolio | | | |
| | Fine Wine 50 Index | Dow Jones Index | US 30 Yr Treas. Bonds Index | Expected Return | | Standard Deviation | |
				per month	per annum	per month	per annum
5 Years from 1998 to 2002	100%	0%	0%	0.2%	3.0%	4.2%	14.7%
5 Years from 1999 to 2003	95%	5%	0%	0.7%	8.4%	3.7%	12.8%
10 Years from 1983 to 1992	26%	74%	0%	1.0%	12.0%	3.6%	12.4%
10 Years from 1993 to 2002	59%	41%	0%	1.1%	13.2%	3.3%	11.5%
10 Years from 1994 to 2003	73%	27%	0%	1.1%	13.2%	3.6%	12.5%
11 Years from 1993 to 2003	67%	33%	0%	1.1%	13.2%	3.4%	11.6%
20 Years from 1983 to 2002	58%	42%	0%	1.0%	12.0%	3.1%	10.6%
20 Years from 1984 to 2003	52%	41%	7%	0.9%	10.8%	2.8%	9.8%
21 Years from 1983 to 2003	91%	9%	0%	1.0%	12.0%	3.7%	12.7%

APPENDIX 23
RISK FREE INVESTMENT VS. OPTIMAL RISK-RETURN EFFICIENT PORTFOLIO RESULTS FOR UK & US DATA INCORPORATING 2003 FROM 1983 TO 2003

Figures in bold represent the preferred investment in the risk free rate as opposed to an investment in either Fine Wine or Equities

Observation Period	3-M LIBOR Risk Free Rate		UK Data Optimal Risk-Return Efficient Portfolio Expected Return		Standard Deviation	
	per month	per annum	per month	per annum	per month	per annum
5 Years from 1998 to 2002	**0.5%**	**5.6%**	0.2%	3.0%	4.2%	14.7%
5 Years from 1999 to 2003	0.4%	4.4%	0.7%	8.4%	3.8%	13.1%
10 Years from 1983 to 1992	1.0%	11.5%	1.2%	14.1%	5.3%	18.4%
10 Years from 1993 to 2002	0.6%	7.3%	1.3%	15.0%	4.6%	15.9%
10 Years from 1994 to 2003	0.5%	5.4%	1.1%	13.8%	4.6%	15.8%
11 Years from 1993 to 2003	0.5%	5.5%	1.1%	13.2%	4.1%	14.2%
20 Years from 1983 to 2002	0.8%	9.4%	1.0%	12.0%	3.7%	12.7%
20 Years from 1984 to 2003	0.7%	8.2%	0.9%	10.8%	3.2%	11.1%
21 Years from 1983 to 2003	0.7%	8.3%	1.0%	11.8%	3.9%	13.7%

Observation Period	3-M DEPOSIT Risk Free Rate		US Data Optimal Risk-Return Expected Return		Efficient Portfolio Standard Deviation	
	per month	per annum	per month	per annum	per month	per annum
5 Years from 1998 to 2002	**0.4%**	**4.7%**	0.2%	3.0%	4.2%	14.7%
5 Years from 1999 to 2003	0.3%	3.8%	0.7%	8.4%	3.7%	12.8%
10 Years from 1983 to 1992	0.6%	7.8%	1.0%	12.0%	3.6%	12.4%
10 Years from 1993 to 2002	0.4%	4.7%	1.1%	13.2%	3.3%	11.5%
10 Years from 1994 to 2003	0.4%	4.4%	1.1%	13.2%	3.6%	12.5%
11 Years from 1993 to 2003	0.4%	4.3%	1.1%	13.2%	3.4%	11.6%
20 Years from 1983 to 2002	0.5%	6.4%	1.0%	12.0%	3.1%	10.6%
20 Years from 1984 to 2003	0.5%	5.8%	0.9%	10.8%	2.8%	9.8%
21 Years from 1983 to 2003	0.5%	5.9%	1.0%	12.0%	3.7%	12.7%

145

APPENDIX 24
MAXIMUM-RETURN PORTFOLIO RESULTS FOR UK & US DATA INCORPORATING 2003 DATA FROM 1983 TO 2003

Maximum-Return Portfolio Results For Fine Wine, Equities & Government Bonds

UK Data

| Observation Period | Weights | | | Maximum-Return Portfolio | | | |
| | Fine Wine 50 Index | FTSE 100 Index | UK Govt. Bonds Index | Expected Return | | Standard Deviation | |
				per month	per annum	per month	per annum
5 Years from 1998 to 2002	100%	0%	0%	0.2%	3.0%	4.2%	14.7%
5 Years from 1999 to 2003	100%	0%	0%	0.7%	8.6%	3.9%	13.4%
10 Years from 1983 to 1992	0%	100%	0%	1.2%	14.1%	5.3%	18.4%
10 Years from 1993 to 2002	100%	0%	0%	1.3%	15.0%	4.6%	15.9%
10 Years from 1994 to 2003	100%	0%	0%	1.1%	13.8%	4.6%	15.8%
11 Years from 1993 to 2003	100%	0%	0%	1.2%	13.9%	4.4%	15.4%
20 Years from 1983 to 2002	100%	0%	0%	1.0%	12.3%	4.0%	13.9%
20 Years from 1984 to 2003	100%	0%	0%	1.0%	11.5%	4.0%	13.9%
21 Years from 1983 to 2003	100%	0%	0%	1.0%	11.8%	3.9%	13.7%

US Data

| Observation Period | Weights | | | Maximum-Return Portfolio | | | |
| | Fine Wine 50 Index | Dow Jones Index | US 30 Yr Treas. Bonds Index | Expected Return | | Standard Deviation | |
				per month	per annum	per month	per annum
5 Years from 1998 to 2002	100%	0%	0%	0.2%	3.0%	4.2%	14.7%
5 Years from 1999 to 2003	100%	0%	0%	0.7%	8.6%	3.9%	13.4%
10 Years from 1983 to 1992	0%	100%	0%	1.1%	12.8%	4.6%	16.0%
10 Years from 1993 to 2002	100%	0%	0%	1.3%	15.0%	4.6%	15.9%
10 Years from 1994 to 2003	100%	0%	0%	1.1%	13.8%	4.6%	15.8%
11 Years from 1993 to 2003	100%	0%	0%	1.2%	13.9%	4.4%	15.4%
20 Years from 1983 to 2002	100%	0%	0%	1.0%	12.3%	4.0%	13.9%
20 Years from 1984 to 2003	0%	100%	0%	1.0%	11.9%	4.6%	16.0%
21 Years from 1983 to 2003	0%	100%	0%	1.0%	12.3%	4.5%	15.8%

146

APPENDIX 25
MINIMUM-RISK PORTFOLIO RESULTS FOR UK & US DATA INCORPORATING 2003 DATA FROM 1983 TO 2003

Minimum-Risk Portfolio Results For Fine Wine, Equities & Government Bonds

UK Data

| Observation Period | Weights | | | Minimum-Risk Portfolio | | | |
| | Fine Wine 50 | FTSE 100 | UK Govt. Bonds | Expected Return | | Standard Deviation | |
	Index	Index	Index	per month	per annum	per month	per annum
5 Years from 1998 to 2002	6%	20%	74%	0.0%	0.0%	1.2%	4.3%
5 Years from 1999 to 2003	9%	11%	80%	(0.1%)	(1.2%)	1.1%	3.8%
10 Years from 1983 to 1992	27%	0%	73%	0.3%	3.6%	1.8%	6.1%
10 Years from 1993 to 2002	8%	5%	87%	0.2%	2.4%	1.4%	4.8%
10 Years from 1994 to 2003	9%	7%	84%	0.1%	1.2%	1.3%	4.7%
11 Years from 1993 to 2003	11%	7%	82%	0.2%	2.4%	1.4%	4.7%
20 Years from 1983 to 2002	18%	4%	78%	0.3%	3.6%	1.6%	5.7%
20 Years from 1984 to 2003	13%	1%	86%	0.2%	2.4%	1.6%	5.6%
21 Years from 1983 to 2003	20%	5%	75%	0.3%	3.6%	1.6%	5.6%

US Data

| Observation Period | Weights | | | Minimum-Risk Portfolio | | | |
| | Fine Wine 50 | Dow Jones | US 30 Yr Treas. Bonds | Expected Return | | Standard Deviation | |
	Index	Index	Index	per month	per annum	per month	per annum
5 Years from 1998 to 2002	0%	0%	100%	0.0%	(0.3%)	0.3%	1.1%
5 Years from 1999 to 2003	0%	0%	100%	0.0%	0.1%	0.4%	1.3%
10 Years from 1983 to 1992	0%	2%	98%	0.0%	0.0%	0.3%	1.0%
10 Years from 1993 to 2002	0%	0%	100%	0.0%	(0.3%)	0.3%	1.1%
10 Years from 1994 to 2003	1%	0%	99%	0.0%	0.0%	0.3%	1.2%
11 Years from 1993 to 2003	2%	0%	98%	0.0%	0.0%	0.3%	1.2%
20 Years from 1983 to 2002	1%	1%	98%	0.0%	0.0%	0.3%	1.0%
20 Years from 1984 to 2003	1%	1%	98%	0.0%	0.0%	0.3%	1.1%
21 Years from 1983 to 2003	1%	1%	98%	0.0%	0.0%	0.3%	1.1%

147

APPENDIX 26
SHARPE RATIO RESULTS FOR UK & US DATA
INCORPORATING 2003 DATA FROM 1983 TO 2003

Sharpe Ratio Results For Fine Wine, Equities & Government Bonds

	UK Data
Observation Period	**Fine Wine 50 Index/**
	FTSE 100 Index/
	UK Govt. Bonds Index

Observation Period	Value
5 Years from 1998 to 2002	(0.05)
5 Years from 1999 to 2003	0.09
10 Years from 1983 to 1992	0.04
10 Years from 1993 to 2002	0.14
10 Years from 1994 to 2003	0.15
11 Years from 1993 to 2003	0.16
20 Years from 1983 to 2002	0.06
20 Years from 1984 to 2003	0.07
21 Years from 1983 to 2003	0.07

Please note that for each observation period the Sharpe Ratio for a portfolio consisting of only financial assets i.e. equities & bonds is lower than the Sharpe Ratio for a portfolio consisting of Fine Wine & financial assets as shown in Appendix 14

	US Data
Observation Period	**Fine Wine 50 Index/**
	Dow Jones Index/
	US 30 Yr Treas. Bonds Index

Observation Period	Value
5 Years from 1998 to 2002	(0.03)
5 Years from 1999 to 2003	0.10
10 Years from 1983 to 1992	0.10
10 Years from 1993 to 2002	0.21
10 Years from 1994 to 2003	0.20
11 Years from 1993 to 2003	0.22
20 Years from 1983 to 2002	0.15
20 Years from 1984 to 2003	0.15
21 Years from 1983 to 2003	0.14

Please note that for each observation period the Sharpe Ratio for a portfolio consisting of Fine Wine & financial assets i.e. equities & bonds for the UK data (as above) is lower than that for tl corresponding US data. This in turn implies that for the US data the Sharpe Ratio for a portfolio consisting of only financial assets would be lower than the Sharpe Ratio for a portfolio consisting of Fine Wine & financial assets

148

APPENDIX 27
BETA VALUE RESULTS FOR UK & US DATA
INCORPORATING 2003 DATA FROM 1983 TO 2003

Sharpe Ratio Results For Fine Wine, Equities & Government Bonds

Observation Period	UK Data Fine Wine 50 Index/ FTSE 100 Index/ UK Govt. Bonds Index	
5 Years from 1998 to 2002	(0.05)	Please note that for each observation period
5 Years from 1999 to 2003	0.09	the Sharpe Ratio for a portfolio consisting of
10 Years from 1983 to 1992	0.04	only financial assets i.e. equities & bonds is
10 Years from 1993 to 2002	0.14	lower than the Sharpe Ratio for a portfolio
10 Years from 1994 to 2003	0.15	consisting of Fine Wine & financial assets
11 Years from 1993 to 2003	0.16	as shown in Appendix 14
20 Years from 1983 to 2002	0.06	
20 Years from 1984 to 2003	0.07	
21 Years from 1983 to 2003	0.07	

Observation Period	US Data Fine Wine 50 Index/ Dow Jones Index/ US 30 Yr Treas. Bonds Index	
5 Years from 1998 to 2002	(0.03)	Please note that for each observation period
5 Years from 1999 to 2003	0.10	the Sharpe Ratio for a portfolio consisting of
10 Years from 1983 to 1992	0.10	Fine Wine & financial assets i.e. equities & bonds
10 Years from 1993 to 2002	0.21	for the UK data (as above) is lower than that for tl
10 Years from 1994 to 2003	0.20	corresponding US data. This in turn implies that
11 Years from 1993 to 2003	0.22	for the US data the Sharpe Ratio for a portfolio
20 Years from 1983 to 2002	0.15	consisting of only financial assets would be lower
20 Years from 1984 to 2003	0.15	than the Sharpe Ratio for a portfolio consisting of
21 Years from 1983 to 2003	0.14	Fine Wine & financial assets

APPENDIX 28
CAPM RESULTS FOR UK & US DATA INCORPORATING 2003 DATA FROM 1983 TO 2003

CAPM Results For Fine Wine & Equities Only

Observation Period	UK Data				
	CAPM Expected Return		Fine Wine 50 Index Expected Return		% Change
	per month	per annum	per month	per annum	
5 Years from 1998 to 2002	0.6%	6.7%	0.2%	3.0%	(55.5%)
5 Years from 1999 to 2003	0.4%	4.2%	0.7%	8.6%	105.5%
10 Years from 1983 to 1992	1.0%	11.6%	0.8%	9.5%	(17.5%)
10 Years from 1993 to 2002	0.6%	7.2%	1.3%	15.0%	107.8%
10 Years from 1994 to 2003	0.4%	5.3%	1.1%	13.8%	157.9%
11 Years from 1993 to 2003	0.5%	5.5%	1.2%	13.9%	154.2%
20 Years from 1983 to 2002	0.8%	9.4%	1.0%	12.3%	31.3%
20 Years from 1984 to 2003	0.7%	8.2%	1.0%	11.5%	40.7%
21 Years from 1983 to 2003	0.7%	8.3%	1.0%	11.8%	42.5%

Observation Period	US Data				
	CAPM Expected Return		Fine Wine 50 Index Expected Return		% Change
	per month	per annum	per month	per annum	
5 Years from 1998 to 2002	0.4%	4.7%	0.2%	3.0%	(36.9%)
5 Years from 1999 to 2003	0.3%	3.8%	0.7%	8.6%	128.2%
10 Years from 1983 to 1992	0.7%	8.0%	0.8%	9.5%	19.5%
10 Years from 1993 to 2002	0.4%	4.8%	1.3%	15.0%	216.1%
10 Years from 1994 to 2003	0.4%	4.7%	1.1%	13.8%	194.8%
11 Years from 1993 to 2003	0.4%	4.5%	1.2%	13.9%	209.0%
20 Years from 1983 to 2002	0.5%	6.5%	1.0%	12.3%	87.8%
20 Years from 1984 to 2003	0.5%	5.9%	1.0%	11.5%	95.2%
21 Years from 1983 to 2003	0.5%	6.1%	1.0%	11.8%	93.1%

APPENDIX 29
CAPM ANALYSIS FOR UK & US DATA INCORPORATING 2003 DATA FROM 1983 TO 2003

CAPM Analysis For Fine Wine & Equities Only
where it indicates to not invest in the Fine Wine 50 Index, an investment in equities or in the risk free asset is preferred

Observation Period	UK Data CAPM Analysis
5 Years from 1998 to 2002	DO NOT INVEST in FW50 Index: RETURN c.56% < CONTRIBUTION to OVERALL PORTFOLIO RISK
5 Years from 1999 to 2003	INVEST in FW50 Index: RETURN c.105% > CONTRIBUTION to OVERALL PORTFOLIO RISK
10 Years from 1983 to 1992	DO NOT INVEST in FW50 Index: RETURN c.18% < CONTRIBUTION to OVERALL PORTFOLIO RISK
10 Years from 1993 to 2002	INVEST in FW50 Index: RETURN c.108% > CONTRIBUTION to OVERALL PORTFOLIO RISK
10 Years from 1994 to 2003	INVEST in FW50 Index: RETURN c.158% > CONTRIBUTION to OVERALL PORTFOLIO RISK
11 Years from 1993 to 2003	INVEST in FW50 Index: RETURN c.154% > CONTRIBUTION to OVERALL PORTFOLIO RISK
20 Years from 1983 to 2002	INVEST in FW50 Index: RETURN c.31% > CONTRIBUTION to OVERALL PORTFOLIO RISK
20 Years from 1984 to 2003	INVEST in FW50 Index: RETURN c.41% > CONTRIBUTION to OVERALL PORTFOLIO RISK
21 Years from 1983 to 2003	INVEST in FW50 Index: RETURN c.43% > CONTRIBUTION to OVERALL PORTFOLIO RISK

Observation Period	US Data CAPM Analysis
5 Years from 1998 to 2002	DO NOT INVEST in FW50 Index: RETURN c.37% < CONTRIBUTION to OVERALL PORTFOLIO RISK
5 Years from 1999 to 2003	INVEST in FW50 Index: RETURN c.128% > CONTRIBUTION to OVERALL PORTFOLIO RISK
10 Years from 1983 to 1992	INVEST in FW50 Index: RETURN c.20% > CONTRIBUTION to OVERALL PORTFOLIO RISK
10 Years from 1993 to 2002	INVEST in FW50 Index: RETURN c.216% > CONTRIBUTION to OVERALL PORTFOLIO RISK
10 Years from 1994 to 2003	INVEST in FW50 Index: RETURN c.195% > CONTRIBUTION to OVERALL PORTFOLIO RISK
11 Years from 1993 to 2003	INVEST in FW50 Index: RETURN c.209% > CONTRIBUTION to OVERALL PORTFOLIO RISK
20 Years from 1983 to 2002	INVEST in FW50 Index: RETURN c.88% > CONTRIBUTION to OVERALL PORTFOLIO RISK
20 Years from 1984 to 2003	INVEST in FW50 Index: RETURN c.95% > CONTRIBUTION to OVERALL PORTFOLIO RISK
21 Years from 1983 to 2003	INVEST in FW50 Index: RETURN c.93% > CONTRIBUTION to OVERALL PORTFOLIO RISK

APPENDIX 30
RISK GRADES RESULTS (I) FOR UK & US DATA INCORPORATING 2003 DATA FROM 1983 TO 2003

Risk Grade Results For Fine Wine & Equities

where 50% is Invested in Fine Wine & 50% in Equities, where FW = Fine Wine 50 Index; FT = FTSE 100 Index; DJ = Dow Jones Index, + = More; - =

Risk Grade Metrics	UK & US Data for 20 Year Period from 1983 to 2002		
	Fine Wine 50 Index	FTSE 100 Index	Dow Jones Index
Risk Grade	69.4	82.6	79.7
Portfolio Risk Grade (50% Fine Wine/50% Equities)	-	54.4	53.5
Undiversified Risk Grade (50% Fine Wine/50% Equities)	-	76.0	74.6
Diversification Benefit (= Risk Grades by which Risk is Reduced)	-	21.6	21.1
% Risk Reduction due to Diversification Benefits	-	28.4%	28.3%
Times Risker compared to Fine Wine 50 Index	-	+1.2	+1.1
Risk Grade by which Equities Exceeds Fine Wine	-	13.2	10.3
% Annual Volatility compared to Fine Wine 50 Index	-	+2.6%	+2.1%
Risk Impact		$RI_{FW} = 13.1$ $RI_{FT} = 19.7$	$RI_{FW} = 13.7$ $RI_{DJ} = 18.8$
% Risk Impact		$\%RI_{FW} = 24.1\%$ $\%RI_{FT} = 36.2\%$	$\%RI_{FW} = 25.5\%$ $\%RI_{DJ} = 35.1\%$

Risk Grade Metrics	UK & US Data for 20 Year Period from 1984 to 2003		
	Fine Wine 50 Index	FTSE 100 Index	Dow Jones Index
Risk Grade	69.6	83.3	79.9
Portfolio Risk Grade (50% Fine Wine/50% Equities)	-	54.8	53.7
Undiversified Risk Grade (50% Fine Wine/50% Equities)	-	76.5	74.8
Diversification Benefit (= Risk Grades by which Risk is Reduced)	-	21.7	21.1
% Risk Reduction due to Diversification Benefits	-	28.4%	28.2%
Times Risker compared to Fine Wine 50 Index	-	+1.2	+1.1
Risk Grade by which Equities Exceeds Fine Wine	-	13.7	10.3
% Annual Volatility compared to Fine Wine 50 Index	-	+2.7%	+2.1%
Risk Impact		$RI_{FW} = 13.2$ $RI_{FT} = 20$	$RI_{FW} = 13.8$ $RI_{DJ} = 18.9$
% Risk Impact		$\%RI_{FW} = 24\%$ $\%RI_{FT} = 36.5\%$	$\%RI_{FW} = 25.6\%$ $\%RI_{DJ} = 35.2\%$

APPENDIX 31
RISK GRADES RESULTS (II) FOR UK DATA
INCORPORATING 2003 DATA FROM 1983 TO 2003

Risk Grade Results For Fine Wine & Equities
where 75% is Invested in Fine Wine & 25% in Equities

Risk Grade Metrics	UK & US Data for 20 Year Period from 1983 to 2002		
	Fine Wine 50 Index	FTSE 100 Index	Dow Jones Index
Risk Grade	69.4	82.6	79.7
Portfolio Risk Grade (75% Fine Wine/25% Equities)	-	56.3	56.2
Undiversified Risk Grade (75% Fine Wine/25% Equities)	-	72.7	72.0
Diversification Benefit (= Risk Grades by which Risk is Reduced)	-	16.4	15.8

Risk Grade Metrics	UK & US Data for 20 Year Period from 1984 to 2003		
	Fine Wine 50 Index	FTSE 100 Index	Dow Jones Index
Risk Grade	69.6	83.3	79.9
Portfolio Risk Grade (75% Fine Wine/25% Equities)	-	56.6	56.4
Undiversified Risk Grade (75% Fine Wine/25% Equities)	-	73.0	72.2
Diversification Benefit (= Risk Grades by which Risk is Reduced)	-	16.4	15.8

Risk Grade Metrics	UK & US Data for 21 Year Period from 1983 to 2003		
	Fine Wine 50 Index	FTSE 100 Index	Dow Jones Index
Risk Grade	68.4	82.2	78.8
Portfolio Risk Grade (75% Fine Wine/25% Equities)	-	55.7	55.6
Undiversified Risk Grade (75% Fine Wine/25% Equities)	-	71.8	71.0
Diversification Benefit (= Risk Grades by which Risk is Reduced)	-	16.1	15.4

APPENDIX 32
RISK GRADES RESULTS (III) FOR UK DATA INCORPORATING 2003 DATA FROM 1983 TO 2003

Risk Grade Results For Fine Wine & Equities
where 25% is Invested in Fine Wine & 75% in Equities

Risk Grade Metrics	UK & US Data for 20 Year Period from 1983 to 2002		
	Fine Wine 50 Index	FTSE 100 Index	Dow Jones Index
Risk Grade	69.4	82.6	79.7
Portfolio Risk Grade (25% Fine Wine/75% Equities)	-	64.6	62.7
Undiversified Risk Grade (25% Fine Wine/75% Equities)	-	79.3	77.1
Diversification Benefit (= Risk Grades by which Risk is Reduced)	-	14.7	14.4

Risk Grade Metrics	UK & US Data for 20 Year Period from 1984 to 2003		
	Fine Wine 50 Index	FTSE 100 Index	Dow Jones Index
Risk Grade	69.6	83.3	79.9
Portfolio Risk Grade (25% Fine Wine/75% Equities)	-	67.9	62.9
Undiversified Risk Grade (25% Fine Wine/75% Equities)	-	79.8	77.3
Diversification Benefit (= Risk Grades by which Risk is Reduced)	-	11.9	14.4

Risk Grade Metrics	UK & US Data for 21 Year Period from 1983 to 2003		
	Fine Wine 50 Index	FTSE 100 Index	Dow Jones Index
Risk Grade	68.4	82.2	78.8
Portfolio Risk Grade (25% Fine Wine/75% Equities)	-	64.3	62.1
Undiversified Risk Grade (25% Fine Wine/75% Equities)	-	78.7	76.2
Diversification Benefit (= Risk Grades by which Risk is Reduced)	-	14.4	14.1

REFERENCES

BOOKS

Beatty, J. *The World According To Drucker.* London: Orion Business, 1st Edition, 1998.

Berman, E. *Return is Only Half the Equation.* New York: The RiskMetrics Group, 1st Edition, 2000.

Bodie, Z. and Kane, A., and Marcus, A.J. *Investments.* New York: McGraw-Hill/Irwin, 5th Edition, 2002.

Campbell, J.Y., and Viceira, L.M. *Strategic Asset Allocation: Portfolio Choice for Long-Term Investors.* New York: Oxford University Press Inc., 1st Edition, 2002.

Cuthbertson, K., and Nitzsche. *Investments: Spot and Derivatives Markets.* Sussex: John Wiley and Sons Ltd, 1st Edition, 2001.

Davis, E.P., Steil, B. *Institutional Investors.* Cambridge, Massachusetts, US: The MIT Press, 1st Edition, 2001.

Edgerton, W. *Edgerton's Wine Price File.* U.S.: Wine Technologies, Inc. 16th Edition, 2002.

Faith, N. *Sold: The Rise and Fall of the House of Sotheby.* New York: Macmillan Publishing Company, 1st Edition, 1985.

Ibbotson, R.G., and Brinson, G.P. *Investment Markets: Gaining the Performance Advantage.* New York: McGraw Hill, 1st Edition, 1987.

Johnson, H. *The World Atlas of Wine.* New York: Simon and Schuster, 1st Edition, 1971.

Kim, J., Mina, J., Laubsch, A.J., and Lee, A. *RiskGrades^{TM} Technical Document.* New York: The RiskMetrics Group, 2nd Edition, 2000.

Parker, R. *Bordeaux: The Definitive Guide for the Wines Produced Since 1961.* New York: Simon and Schuster, 1st Edition, 1985.

Pickford, J. *Financial Times Mastering Investment.* London: Prentice Hall, 1st Edition, 2002.

Robinson, J. *The Oxford Companion To Wine*. New York: Oxford University Press Inc, 2nd Edition, 1999.

Rush, R.H. *Art as an Investment*. New Jersey: Prentice-Hall, 1st Edition, 1961.

Sokolin, W. *Liquid Assets*. New York: Macmillan, 1st Edition, 1987.

ACADEMIC PAPERS

Ashenfelter, O. "How Auctions Work for Wine and Art." *Journal of Economic Perspectives 3*, 1989, pp. 23–36

Ashenfelter, O., Ashmore, D., and Lalonde, R. *Wine Vintage Quality and the Weather: Bordeaux*. Paper Presented at the Second International Conference of the Vineyard Quantification Society, Verona, Italy, 18–19 February, 1993.

Bailey, M., Muth, R., and Nourse. "A Regression Method for Real Estate Price Index Construction." *Journal of the American Statistical Association 58*, 1963, pp. 933–942.

Bartholomew, J. "Collectibles: State of the Art." *Far Eastern Economic Review 154*, 1991, pp. 37–38.

Baum, J.A.C., and Powell, W.W. "Cultivating an Institutional Ecology of Organisation." *American Journal of Sociology 60*, 1995, pp. 529–538

Baumol, W. "Unnatural Value: Or Art Investment as Floating Crap Game." *American Economic Review 76*, 1986, pp. 10–14.

Benartzi and Thaler. "How Much is Investor Autonomy Worth." *National Bureau of Economic Research*, 2001, 5 pp.

Britten-Jones, M. "Sampling Error in Mean-Variance Efficient Portfolio Weights." *Journal of Finance*, 1999, 12 pp.

Burton, B.J., and Jacobsen, J.P. "Measuring Returns on Investment in Collectables." *Journal of Economic Perspectives 13,* 1999, pp. 193–212.

Burton, B.J., and Jacobsen, J.P. "The Rate of Return on Investment in Wine." *Economic Inquiry 39,* 2001, pp. 337–350.

Byron, R.P., and Ashenfelter, O. "Predicting the Quality of an Unborn Grange." *Economic Record 71,* 1995, pp. 40–53.

Campbell, R. *The Art of Portfolio Diversification.* Maastricht University, 2004.

Cardell, N.S., Kling, J.L., and Petry, G. "Stamp Returns and Economic Factors." *Southern Economic Journal 62:2,* 1995, pp. 411–27.

Chanel, O. "Is Art Market Behaviour Predictable?" *European Economic Review 39,* 1995, pp. 519–27.

Coffman, R.B. "Art Investment and Asymmetrical Information." *Journal of Cultural Economics 15:2,* 1991, pp. 83–94.

Cutler, D.M., Poterba, J.M., and Summers, L.M. "Speculative Dynamics." *Review of Economic Studies 58:3,* 1991, pp. 529–46.

DeBondt, W. "A Portrait of the Individual Investor." *European Economic Review 42,* 1998, pp. 831–844.

Formanek, R. "Why They Collect? : Collectors Reveal Their Motivations." *Journal of Social Behaviour and Personality 6:6,* 1991, pp. 275–286.

Frey, B., and Pommerehne, W. "Art Investment: An Empirical Inquiry." *Southern Economic Journal 56,* 1989, pp. 396–409.

Frey, B.S., and Serna, A. "Der Preis der Kunst." *Kursbuch 99,* 1990, pp. 105–113.

Frey, B.S. "Art Markets and Economics: Introduction." *Journal of Cultural Economics 21:3,* 1997, pp. 165–173.

Ginsburgh, V., and Jeanfils, P. "Long–Term Comovements in International Markets for Paintings." *European Economic Review 39:3–4,* 1995, pp. 538–548.

Goetzmann, W.N. "Accounting for Taste: Art and the Financial Markets over Three Centuries." *American Economic Review 83*, 1993, pp. 1370–1376

Goetzmann, W.N. "The Informational Efficiency of the Art Market." *Managerial Finance 21:6*, 1995, pp. 25–34.

Goetzmann, W.N., and Spiegel, M. "Private Value Components, and the Winner's Curse in an Art Index" *European Economic Review 39*, 1995, pp. 549–555.

Goetzmann, W.N. "How Costly is the Fall from Fashion? Survivorship Bias in the Painting Market." *Economics of the Arts—Selected Essays*, 1996, pp. 71–84.

Goetzmann, W.N., and Kumar, A. "Equity Portfolio Diversification." *National Bureau of Economic Research Working Paper Number 8686*, 2001, 44 pp.

Goldsmith, D. "Transaction Costs and the Theory of Portfolio Selection." *Journal of Finance, Vol. XXXI, No. 4*, 1976, pp. 1127–1140.

Graeser, P. "Rate of Return to Investment in American Antique Furniture." *Southern Economic Journal 59*, 1993, pp. 817–821.

Huberman, G. "Familiarity Breeds Investment." *Review of Financial Studies 14*, 2001, pp. 659–680.

Ibbotson, R.G. "Global Asset Allocation: Philosophy, Process and Performance." *Journal of Investing 9 (1)*, 2000, p. 39.

Jaeger, E. "To Save or Savour: The Rate of Return to Storing Wine." *Journal of Political Economy 89*, 1981, pp. 584–592.

Kane, A. "Coins: Anatomy of a Fad Asset." *Journal of Portfolio Management 1:2*, 1984, pp. 44–51.

Kelly, M. "All their Eggs in One Basket: Portfolio Diversification of US Households." *Journal of Economic Behaviour and Organization 27*, 1995, pp. 87–96.

Krasker, W. "The Rate of Return to Storing Wines." *Journal of Political Economy 87*, 1979, 5 pp.

Kroll, Y., Levy, H., and Rapoport, A. "Experimental Tests of the Separation of Theorem and the Capital Asset Pricing Model." *American Economic Review 78,* 1988, pp. 500–519.

Lee, S.M., and Lerro, A.J. "Optimising the Portfolio Selection for Mutual Funds." *Journal of Finance,* Vol. 28, No.5, 1973, pp. 1087–1102.

Linter, J. "The Valuation of Risky Assets and The Selection of Risky Investments in Stock Portfolios and Capital Budgets." *Review of Economics and Statistics,* Feb., 1965.

Long, M.M., and Schiffman, L.G. "Swatch Fever: An Allegory for Understanding the Paradox of Collecting." *Psychology and Marketing 14:5,* 1997, pp. 495–509.

Markowitz, H.M. "Portfolio Selection." *Journal of Finance 7,* 1952, pp. 77–91.

Markowitz, H.M. "Foundations of Portfolio Theory." *Journal of Finance,* 1991, 24 pp.

Mei, J., and Moses, M. "The All Art Index." *Stern School of Business Publication,* New York University, 2002.

Merton, R. C. "Lifetime Portfolio Selection under Uncertainty: The Continuous-Time Case." *The Review of Economics and Statistics 51,* 1969, pp. 247–257.

Merton, R. C. "An Analytic Derivation of the Efficient Portfolio Frontier." *The Journal of Financial and Quantitative Analysis 7,* 1972, pp 1851–1872

Merton, R. C. "An Intertemporal Capital Asset Pricing Model." *Econometrica 41,* 1973, pp. 867–887.

Merton, R. C. "A Simple Model of Capital Market Equilibrium with Incomplete Information." *Journal of Finance 42,* 1987, pp. 483–510.

Mossin, J. "Equilibrium in a Capital Asset Market." *Econometrica,* Oct., 1966.

Nelson, P.. "Information and Consumer Behaviour." *Journal of Political Economy 78,* 1970, pp. 311–329.

Odean, T. "Do Investors Trade Too Much?" *American Economic Review 89*, 1999, pp. 1279–1298.

Pesando, J.E. "Art as an Investment: The Market for Modern Prints." *American Economic Review 83 (5)*, 1993, pp. 1075–89.

Pompe, J. "An Investment Flash: The Rate of Return for Photographs." *Southern Economic Journal 63:2*, 1996, pp. 488–495.

Rao, H. "The Social Construction of Reputation: 1895–1912." *Strategic Management Journal 15*, 1994, pp. 29–44.

Rode, D. "Portfolio Choice and Perceived Diversification." Working Paper, Department of Social and Decision Sciences, Carnegie Mellon University, 2000.

Shapiro, C. "Premiums for High Quality Products as Returns to Reputations." *Quarterly Journal of Economics 98*, 1983, pp. 659–679.

Sharpe, W.F. "A Simplified Model of Portfolio Analysis." *Management Science*, Jan., 1963.

Sharpe, W.F. "Capital Asset Prices: A Theory of Market Equilibrium under Conditions of Risk." *Journal of Finance 19*, 1964, pp. 425–442.

Weil, R.L. "Do Not Invest in Wine, At Least in the US, Unless You Plan to Drink It, and Maybe Not Even Then, or As An Investment, Wine is No Corker." Paper Presented at the 2nd International Conference of the Vineyard Quantification Society, Verona, Italy, 1993.

NON-ACADEMIC ARTICLES

Bawden, A. "Alternative Investments: Tangible Assets With Less of a String Attached." *Financial Times*, May 25, 2002.

Brown, C. "Art for Money's Sake." *Forbes*, Dec. 5, 1994.

Clowes, G. *The Case For Fine Wine Investment.* Fine Wine Management Company, 2002.

Damato, K. "Finding Funds That Zig When Blue Chips Zag." *The Wall Street Journal*, Jun. 17, 1997.

Davison, A., Boom, G., and Christofolini, P. *The Vintage Wine Fund.* OWC Asset Management, 2003.

Fuhrman, P. "Drinking Your Profits is the Best Revenge." *Forbes*, Vol. 145, Issue 13, Jun., 1990, pp. 270–272.

Grimond, M. "A Vintage Year to Bottle Up Fine Profits in Your Cellar." *Business Day*, Jan. 12, 1998.

Meltzer, P. "Third Quarter Gains Nearly Double Previous Results." *Wine Spectator*, Dec. 31, 1997, pp. 16–17

O'Riley, M.K. "It's a Cellar's Market." *Director*, Jan., 2001.

Peers, A. "Hot Cellars: Wine Prices are Soaring." *Wall Street Journal*, May 2, 1997.

Premier Cru. Premier Cru Fine Wine Investment Ltd., 2002.

Prial, F.J. "Bordeaux Again Leads a High-Price Parade." *New York Times*, Sep. 17, 1997.

Robinson, J., and Boom, G. "Head to Head." *Decanter*, Jan., 2003.

Spurrier, S. "Auction Fever: Can Prices Rise Forever?" *Decanter*, Dec., 1997.

Thomas, M. "Alternative Investing: Wine Collectors Drive Up Prices." *Business News New Jersey (North)*, Jan. 19, 1998

BIBLIOGRAPHY

BOOKS

Alexander, G.J., Sharpe, W.F., and Bailey, J.V. *Fundamentals of Investment.* New Jersey: Prentice-Hall, 3rd Ed., 2001.

Arnold, G. *Corporate Financial Management.* London: Financial Times/ Prentice Hall, 2nd Ed., 2002.

Brealey, R., and Myers, S. *Principles of Corporate Finance.* New York: McGraw-Hill/Irwin, 7th Ed., 2002.

Brook, S. *A Century of Wine: The Story of a Wine Revolution.* London: Octopus Publishing Group Ltd., 1st Ed., 2000.

Clarke, O., and Spurrier, S. *Fine Wine Guide: Wine, Growers and Vintages,* London: Websters, Little, Brown and Company, 2nd Ed., 2001.

Copeland, T., Koller, T., and Murrin, J. *Valuation: Measuring and Managing The Value of Companies.* McKinsey and Company Inc., 3rd Ed., 2002.

Cuthbertson, K., and Nitzsche. *Financial Engineering: Derivatives and Risk Management.* Sussex: John Wiley and Sons Ltd., 1st Ed., 2001.

Dickson, T., and Bickerstaffe, G. *Financial Times Mastering Finance.* London: Prentice-Hall, 2nd Ed., 2002.

Dimson, E., Marsh, P., and Staunton, M. *Triumph of the Optimists: 101 Years of Global Investment Returns.* U.S.: Princeton University Press, 1st Ed., 2002.

Gollier, C. *The Economics of Risk and Time.* Cambridge: MIT Press, MA, US, 2001.

Krishna, V. *Auction Theory,* Academic Press. US: 1st Ed., 2002.

Loftus, S. *Anatomy of the Wine Trade.* London: Sidgwick and Jackson, 1st Ed., 1985.

Markowitz, H.M. *Portfolio Selection: Efficient Diversification of Investments.* New York: Wiley, 2nd Ed., 1991.

Price, P.V. *Curiosities of Wine*. Gloucestershire: Sutton Publishing Ltd., 1st Ed., 2002.

Saunders, M., Lewis, P., and Thornhill, A. *Research Methods for Business Students*. London: Prentice-Hall, 3rd Ed., 2003.

Siegel, J.J. *Stocks for the Long Run*. New York: McGraw-Hill, 3rd Ed., 2002.

Spahni, P. *The International Wine Trade*. Cambridge: Woodhead, 1st Ed., 1995.

Spurrier, S., and Ward, J. *How To Buy Fine Wines: A Practical Guide for The Collector and Connoisseur*. London: Paidon-Christie's Ltd, 1st Ed., 1986.

Vaitilingam, R. *The Financial Times Guide to Using The Financial Pages*. London: Prentice-Hall, 4th Ed., 2001.

Valdez, S. *An Introduction To Global Financial Markets*. US: Palgrave, 3rd Ed., 2000.

Wallace, F., and Cross, G. *The Game of Wine*. US: Doubleday and Co. Inc., 1st Ed., 1976.

Zask, E. *Global Investment Risk Management*. New York: McGraw-Hill, 1st Ed., 1999.

ACADEMIC PAPERS

Barberis, N.C. "Investing for the Long Run when Returns are Predictable." *Journal of Finance 55,* 2000, pp. 225–264.

Bertaut, C.C., and Haliassos, A. "Why Do So Few Hold Stocks?" *Economic Journal 105,* 1995, pp. 1110–1129.

Blake, J., Amat, O., and Dowds, J. "The Drive for Quality: The Impact on Accounting in the Wine Industry." *Journal of Wine Research 9,* 1998, pp. 75–85.

Blattel, H., and Stainless, F.E. *Wine and Price: International Auction Results.* 1997.

Bodie, Z. "Risk of Stocks in the Long Run." *Financial Analysts Journal 51,* 1995, 5 pp.

Campbell, J.Y. "Understanding Risk and Return." *Journal of Political Economy 104,* 1996, pp. 298–345.

Campbell, J.Y., and Viceira, L.M. "Who Should Buy Long-Term Bonds." *Harvard Institute of Economic Research Discussion Paper Number 1895,* 1999, 76 pp.

Campbell, J.Y., and Viceira, L.M. "Who Should Buy Long-Term Bonds." *American Economic Review 91,* 2001, pp. 99–127.

Campbell, J.Y., and Shiller, R.J. "Valuation Ratios and the Long-Run Stock Market Outlook: An Update." *Harvard Institute of Economic Research Working Paper Number 8221,* 2001, 45 pp.

Canner, N., Mankiw, N.G., and Weil, D.N. "An Asset Allocation Puzzle." *American Economic Review 87,* 1997, pp. 181–191.

Cassell, M. "Risk and Return." *Management Accounting,* Oct., 1999, 4 pp.

Cochrane, J.H. "New Facts in Finance." *Economic Perspectives,* 2000, pp. 36–58.

Cochrane, J.H. "Portfolio Advice for a Multifactor World." *Economic Perspectives,* 2000, pp. 59–78.

Elton, E.J., and Gruber, M.J. "The Rationality of Asset Allocation Recommendations." *Journal of Financial and Quantitative Analysis 35,* 2000, pp. 27–41.

Fase, M.M.G. "Purchase of Art: Consumption and Investment." *The Economist 144:4,* 1996, pp. 649–659.

Ferris, S.P., and Makhija, A.K. "Tangible Assets as Investment: A Risk and Return Analysis." *Akron Business and Economic Review 18:3,* 1987, pp. 115–128.

Folwell, R.J., Bales, T.A., and Edwards, C.G. "Cost Economies and Economic Impacts of Pricing and Product Mix Decisions in Premium Table Wine Wineries." *Journal of Wine Research 12,* 2001, pp. 111–124

Foster, W., and Beaujanot, A., and Zuniga, J.I. "Marketing Focus in the Wine Industry." *Journal of Wine Research 13,* 2002, pp. 35–42.

Frey, B.S., and Eichenberger, R. "On the Rate of Return in the Art Market: Survey and Evaluation." *European Economic Review 39:3,* 1995, pp. 529–537.

Frey, B.S., and Eichenberger, R. "On the Return of Art Investment Return Analyses." *Journal of Cultural Economics 19,* 1995, pp. 207–220.

Gennotte, G. 'Optimal Portfolio Choice under Incomplete Information." *Journal of Finance 41,* 1986, pp. 733–746.

Ginsburgh, V. "Absentee Bidders and the Declining Price Anomaly in Wine Auctions." *Journal of Political Economy 106:6,* 1998, pp. 1302–1319.

Glosten, L.R., Jagannathan, R., and Runkle, D. "On the Relation between the Expected Value and the Volatility of the Nominal Excess Return on Stocks." *Journal of Finance 48,* 1993, pp. 1779–1801.

Grossman, S.J., and Shiller, R.J. "The Determinants of the Variability of Stock Market Prices." *American Economic Review 71,* 1981, pp. 222–227.

Grossman, S.J. "Dynamic Asset Allocation and the Informational Efficiency of Markets." *The Journal of Finance,* 1995, pp. 773–787.

Jagannathan, R., Kocherlakota, N.R., McGrattan, E.R., and Scherbina, A. "The Declining US Equity Premium." *National Bureau of Economic Research Working Paper Number 8172,* 2001.

Kandel, S., and Stambaugh, R. "On The Predictability of Stock Returns: An Asset Allocation Perspective." *Journal of Finance 51,* 1996, pp. 385–424.

Lages, L.F. "Marketing Lessons from Wine Exporters: The Development and Application of a Conceptual Framework." *Journal of Wine Research 10,* 1999, pp. 123–132.

Lakonishok, J., Shleifer, A., and Vishny, R.W. "Contrarian Investment, Extrapolation and Risk." *Journal of Finance*, XLIX, 5, 1994, 33 pp.

Lewis, K. "Trying to Explain Home Bias in Equities and Consumption." *Journal of Economic Literature 37*, 1999, pp. 571–608.

Lynch, A.W. "Portfolio Choice and Equity Characteristics: Characterising the Hedging Demands Induced by Return Predictability." *Journal of Financial Economics 62*, 2001, pp. 67–130.

Merton, R. C. and Samuelson, P. A. "Generalised Mean-Variance Tradeoffs for Best Perturbation Corrections to Approximate Portfolio Decisions." *The Journal of Finance 29*, 1974, pp. 27–40.

Pastor, L. "Portfolio Selection and Asset Pricing Models." *Journal of Finance 55*, 2000, 44 pp.

Roberts, P.W., and Reagans, R. "Market Experience: Consumer Attention and Price-Quality Relationships for New World Wines in the US Market from 1987 to 1999." *Academy of Management Proceedings*, 2001, 6 pp.

Rubinstein, M. "Rational Markets: Yes or No? The Affirmative Case." *Financial Analysts Journal*, 2001, pp. 15–29.

Stein, J. "Rational Capital Budgeting in an Irrational World." *The Journal of Business*, 1996, 4 pp.

Statman, M. "How Many Stocks Make a Diversified Portfolio." *Journal of Financial and Quantitative Analysis 22*, 1987, pp. 353–364.

Thaler, R.H. "Mental Accounting and Consumer Choice." *Marketing Science 4*, 1985, pp. 199–214.

Weil, P. "The Equity Premium Puzzle and the Risk-Free Rate Puzzle." *Journal of Monetary Economics 24*, 1989, pp. 401–21.

Wittwer, G., and Anderson, K. "Accounting for Growth in the Australian Wine Industry." *Australian Economic Review 34*, 2001, pp. 179–189.

Non-Academic Articles

Athineos, D., and Flanagan, W.G. "Grape Expectations." *Forbes*, Vol 157, Issue 8, April 1996, 1996, 2 pp.

Bartram, P. "Liquid Investments." *Director*, Vol 54, Issue 1, Aug. 2000, p. 88.

Baldock, F. "Vintage Investments." *Canadian Business*, Vol. 70, No. 4, Apr. 1997, p. 135.

Beard, A., and Roberts, A. "Global Investing: Wine Investor Plants its Faith in the Soil." *Financial Times*, Sep. 25, 2001.

Bennett, H. "Put Your Money Where Your Mouth Is: Invest In Wine." *Accountancy*, Jan. 1980.

Boom, G. "Traded on the Grapevine: A More Efficient Market in Claret." *The Economist*, Jan. 10.

Bredenberg, J. "Buying Luxuries on a Budget." *Black Enterprise*, Vol 29, No. 3, Oct. 1998, pp. 155–157.

Caudron, S. "$32,000…Sold!" *Industry Week*, Vol. 247, Issue 14, Jul. 1998, 2 pp.

Chatzky, J.S. "Buy Low, Drink High: How to Invest in Wine." *Money*, Vol. 27, Issue 8, 1998, p. 144.

Clarke, P. "Why Potential Investors Must Do Their Homework." *Financial Times*, Jan. 19, 2002.

Clarke, P. "Drinks Investment: Right Wine, Wrong Price." *Financial Times*, Feb. 16, 2002.

Clarke, P. "Global Investing: Handsome Gains From The Humble Grape." *Financial Times*, Jun. 28, 2002.

Clarke, P. "Global Investing: Turning Wine and Water Into A Quick Profit." *Financial Times*, Sep. 27, 2002.

Clements, J. "Recipe for Successful Investing: First Mix Assets Well." *The Wall Street Journal*, Oct. 6, 1993.

Clements, J. "The Right Mix: Fine-Tuning a Portfolio." *The Wall Street Journal*, Jul. 23, 1996.

Climo, C. "Investing in Wine." *Money* (Australia), Oct. 2002, pp. 38–39.

Coffey, B. "Drink it Up." *Forbes*, Dec. 2000, Vol. 166, No. 15, pp. 336–337.

Corrigan, A. "Passionate Debate." *Cairns Post*, Dec. 17, 2002..

Corrigan, A. "Liquid Assets." *Brisbane News*, Feb. 5, 2003.

DeBondt, R. "The Value of Wine." *The Greenville Journal*, May 11–17, 2001.

Eaglesham, J. "Wine Company that Duped Investors Wound Up." *Financial Times*, Feb. 6, 2002..

Echikson, W. "Wine War." *Business Week,* Issue 3747, Sep. 2001, 7 pp.

Francis, C. "Sick of Shares? Try Woods or Wine." *The Sunday Times*, Jun. 8, 2003.

Gascoigne, C. "Consumable Classics: By No Means Just For Drinking." *Financial Times*, Mar. 8, 2000.

Goldberg, H.G. "2002–2003 U.S. Auctions." *Decanter*, Jan. 2002–Jun. 2003.

Grubb, P. "The Gilt-Edged Grape." ˆ Vol 3, No. 2, May 1979.

Harper, L., and Jensen, E. "Investors Bet on Rare Bubbly." *The Wall Street Journal*, Feb. 1998.

Hendery, S. "BRL Hardy Accepts $2bn to Form World's Biggest Vinter." *New Zealand Herald*, Jan. 18, 2003.

Hendery, S. "Internet Wine Sale Aims to Lift Prices." *New Zealand Herald*, Mar. 1, 2003.

Laube, J. "Collecting vs. Investing." *Wine Spectator*, Jul. 31, 1997.

Lee, J.C. "Wine: Drink Later—Wine Futures." *Far Eastern Review,* May 2002..

Losh, C. "Tipping the Bottle." *Wine*, May, 2003.

Matterson, H. 'Enjoy a Cab Savvy Way." *The Australian*, Feb. 22, 2003.

McManus, G. "Wine Markets Expand." *NZ Business,* Vol. 12, Issue 8, Sep. 1998, 6 pp.

McGinty, A. "Bottoms Up: Wine Offers Upside to Investors." *Canadian Business,* Oct. 2002, Vol. 75, Issue 20, p. 22.

Newcomb, P. "Grape Expectations: Model Portfolio." *Forbes,* Vol 169, Issue 13, June 2002, pp. 238–239

Parker, R. "Playing the Rating Game." *The Economist*, Sep. 16, 1999.

Pawlyna. A. "Appreciating Liquid Assets." *Asian Business,* Jul. 1995.

Peterson, T. "Collecting Wine for Profit and Fun." *Business Week,* Apr. 2002, 1 p.

Prial, F.J. "California Cabernets Join the Gold Rush." *New York Times,* Jan. 7, 1998.

Rachman, G. "The Globe in the Glass." *The Economist,* Dec. 16, 1999.

Reilly, J.K. "Cellar's Market." *Fortune,* Vol. 147, No. 2, Feb. 2003, p. 135.

Robinson, J. "The Brand's the Thing." *The Economist,* Dec. 1999.

Robinson, J.. "Wine Investment: How to Take a Punt and Make a Mint." *Financial Times,* April 8, 2000.

Robinson, J. "Fine Wine Investment in the 1990s." *The Oxford Companion To Wine,* Oxford University Press Inc, New York, 2nd Edition, 1999.

Rose, A. "The Price Puzzle." *The Economist,* Dec. 16, 1999.

Rose, A. "2002–2003 UK Auctions." *Decanter*, Jan. 2002–Jun. 2003.

Schmidt, L. "Investors Want to be in the Red." *Business Review Weekly,* Feb. 4, 2000.

Smith, G.N. "Drink the Dividends." *FW,* Vol. 164, No. 6, Feb. 1995, p. 12.

Stein, J. "Tales from the FAR Side." *The Economist,* Nov. 16, 1996, p. 8.

Stimpfig, J. "Guess What? Bordeaux is Best." *Decanter,* May 2003.

Stimpfig, J. "Buying Burgundy." *Decanter*, Mar. 2003.

Stimpfig, J. "A New Player in the Wine Investment Fund Market." *Decanter*, Feb. 2003.

Stimpfig, J. "Fine Wine Market Sends Out Mixed Messages." *Decanter*, Jan. 2002.

Tanzer, S. "Grape Juice: America's Newest White-Collar Killers, and Other Wine Predictions." *Forbes*, Vol. 157, No. 9, May 1999, pp. 45–48.

Walker, D.M. "Vintage Stock." *The Age*, Oct. 4, 1999.

Woods, K. "Wine Success is Not Just in the Bottle." *Herald and Weekly Times*, Dec. 11, 2002.

Zacharia, J. "Vintage Advice." *Fortune*, Oct. 27, Vol. 136, No. 8, 1997, 2 pp.

Zwick, S. "Another Name for Liquidity." *Time South Pacific*, Issue 1, Jan. 2002, p. 53.

INTERNET SITES

Stock Exchanges and Central Banks
London Stock Exchange   http://www.londonstockexchange.com
New York Stock Exchange   http://www.nyse.com
Bank of England   http://www.bankofengland.com
European Central Bank   http://www.ecb.int
Federal Reserve Board (US)   http://bog.frb.fed.us
Financial Service Authority   http://www.fsa.gov.uk

Newspapers and News Agencies
Financial Times   http://www.ft.com
The Economist   http://www.economist.com
Wall Street Journal   http://www.wsj.com
Bloomberg   http://www.bloomberg.com
Reuters   http://www.reuters.com

RiskGrades™   http://www.riskgrades.com
RiskMetrics   http://www.riskmetrics.com

Wine Periodicals
    Decanter   http://www.decanter.com
    Wine Advocate   http://www.erobertparker.com
    Wine Magazine (UK)   http://www.winemagazine.co.uk
    Wine Magazine (US)   http://www.wineontheweb.com
    Wine Spectator   http://www.winespectator.com

Auction Houses
    Sotheby's   http://www.sothebys.com
    Christie's   http://www.christies.com

    Sotheby's and Christies Finest and Rarest Wines Auction
    Catalogues 1960–2002

Resources For Fine Wine Investors

Appraisals

William Edgerton, Box 1007, Darien Ct. 06820, (203) 655-0566
appraisals@brentwoodwine.com

Buying and Selling Fine Wines

www.ackerwines.com
www.brentwoodwine.com
www.cellar.com
www.christies.com (212) 636-2270
www.finewinemanagement.co.uk
www.hitimewine.com
www.kensingtonsfinewine.com (312) 836-7850
www.klwine.com (877) 559-4637
www.morellwineauctions.com (212) 307-4200
www.sothebys.com
www.finfolio.com
www.winebid.com
www.zachysauction.com (914) 448-3026

Temperature and Humidity Controlled Wine Storage

www.silentcellar.com (866) 231-9463
www.wineappreciation.com (800) 231-9463
www.winehardware.com   (800) 616-9463
www.wineware.co.uk   (0) 1903 723557
www.westpalmwines.com (813) 241-5857

INDEX